The Elephant i

The Elephant in the Staffroom is the survival guide that every busy teacher needs for practical advice on teacher wellbeing. Written in an informal, conversational style, the book is divided into 40 bite-size chunks, covering a range of essential topics from understanding and avoiding burnout to developing successful working patterns – and even surviving the school holidays!

Complemented by a host of top tips, the book focuses on five key themes:

- the psychology of the teacher
- teacher identity
- emotional and physical energy
- keeping focused and investing in yourself
- colleagues, students and inspection.

Chapters are designed to be easily dipped in and out of, with each exploring the unique nature of the teaching profession and how to cope with, and conquer, a variety of stress triggers and psychological aspects of teaching – 'elephants' in the staffroom – to survive and succeed.

Written by a head of department with over 20 years of classroom experience, this essential guide offers a wealth of practical advice on stress, work–life balance and organisation, and is a must-read for practising teachers.

Chris Eyre is Lead Practitioner for Teaching and Learning, and Curriculum Manager for Religious Studies and Philosophy, at Stoke-on-Trent Sixth Form College, UK.

The Elephant in the Staffroom

How to reduce stress and improve teacher wellbeing

Chris Eyre

Routledge
Taylor & Francis Group

LONDON AND NEW YORK

First published 2017
by Routledge
2 Park Square, Milton Park, Abingdon, Oxon OX14 4RN

and by Routledge
711 Third Avenue, New York, NY 10017

Routledge is an imprint of the Taylor & Francis Group, an informa business

© 2017 Chris Eyre

The right of Chris Eyre to be identified as author of this work has been
asserted by him in accordance with sections 77 and 78 of the Copyright,
Designs and Patents Act 1988.

British Library Cataloguing in Publication Data
A catalogue record for this book is available from the British Library

Library of Congress Cataloging-in-Publication Data
Names: Eyre, Chris, author.
Title: The elephant in the staffroom : a guide to teacher wellbeing /
    Chris Eyre.
Description: New York : Routledge, 2017. | Includes bibliographical
    references and index.
Identifiers: LCCN 2016016525 (print) | LCCN 2016030910 (ebook) |
    ISBN 9781138681477 (hardback) | ISBN 9781138681484 (pbk.) |
    ISBN 9781315545790 (ebook)
Subjects: LCSH: Teachers—Job satisfaction. | Teachers—Mental health. |
    Effective teaching.
Classification: LCC LB2840 .E97 2017 (print) | LCC LB2840 (ebook) |
    DDC 371.102—dc23
LC record available at https://lccn.loc.gov/2016016525

ISBN: 978-1-138-68147-7 (hbk)
ISBN: 978-1-138-68148-4 (pbk)
ISBN: 978-1-315-54579-0 (ebk)

Typeset in Celeste and Optima
by Apex CoVantage, LLC

Contents

PART 3
Energy   **89**

PART 4
Focus   **133**

PART 5
The others   **179**

Preface

The title of this book is no longer fully relevant. The good news is that stress and wellbeing are no longer complete elephants in the staff-room; they are beginning to enter conversations in leadership meetings, in the media and even in the government itself. At the time this book was conceived and writing began, that was not the case. We all knew the problems were there, but it is far easier, and makes for better headlines, if we focus on things that can be easily changed; hence the lively debates on all sorts of other things. Even now progress is slow and we are in a system that causes much unnecessary stress, wearing out good teachers to the point that they leave. Given that this is unlikely to change anytime soon – there are no magic bullets on the system level – it falls to each of us to take responsibility for our own wellbeing and put things in place that enable us both to survive and to flourish. This is both a psychological and practical issue; hence this book looks at both how we think as teachers and also the practical organisational steps that make us more efficient.

The first part of the book is perhaps a little gloomy, outlining the situation as it stands, but it is necessary that we understand the problems before looking at solutions. What follows through three main themes – identity, energy and focus – is a series of chapters looking at both the psychological and the practical aspects of managing stress in and out of the classroom. Each chapter has some questions at the end that are prompts for reflection and will hopefully help you to continue the conversation with yourself or others.

As well as continuing to work as a full time teacher during the process of thinking and writing, I have spoken to lots of teachers in the last few years and have read the thoughts of many more. Undoubtedly there are many people who have unconsciously influenced what has been written. I hope that I have been faithful to the story of your journey and that what I have written will help.

My aim in writing is to help others on the journey, acknowledging that we all have good and bad days and we must hang in there both for the sake of our students and, more importantly, our own health. If this helps people to face their daily teaching with a renewed enthusiasm or prevents a few people from going off sick with stress, or taking it out on their nearest and dearest, then it will be worthwhile. Let's acknowledge the huge stress and wellbeing elephant and, more importantly, continue the conversation about it!

Acknowledgements

Thank you to Cath, Richard and Iona for your love and support and for believing in me more than I believe in myself. To colleagues past and present, thank you.

Chapter 1

Three things to remember when you forget everything else

It is true of most jobs that you don't really understand the difficulties and pressures unless you have actually done the job or have lived with someone who has. I occasionally have pipe dreams of owning a small café or possibly improving my fitness by becoming a postman. Yet these brief fantasies usually involve a steady stream of customers coming into the shop, never too many. It is always possible to serve them quickly, I've always got exactly what they want, and they're always happy. In my life as a postman it is always sunny and all packages are correctly addressed. There are no hailstorms, angry dogs or packages that don't fit into letter boxes.

This brings us to the outsiders' view of teaching. In this world there are 6- or 7-hour working days, and you get 13 weeks of vacation every year. The students are always attentive and appreciative – an idea gained from watching *Dead Poets Society* several times, or perhaps from soap operas in which teacher characters are rarely seen preparing lessons, manage to get to the pub each night and are usually able to meet up with another character for an affair in a free period.

However, in the interests of balance, it is equally true that some people within teaching are convinced that they suffer the greatest hardships known to man. The truth, as ever, lies between these extremes. Here are the three most important things to remember about teaching.

1. It could be worse

A little knowledge is a dangerous thing. Often as teachers we lose perspective. Many of us have never really left education. We went to school, then to college and university, and apart from that brief summer job in the shop, our whole world has been the world of education. Some of us don't stop to think that there are some pretty unpleasant jobs out there, many of which are paid far less than we earn. On a bad day I remind myself that my father went down a mine every day for over 20 years and on more than one occasion saw colleagues carried out dead or seriously injured. He worked far harder in a physical sense than I will ever do, risked life and limb and earned less than the teachers of his day. Consider the paramedic attending a road traffic accident or the nurse working a Friday night in A & E. How about the people who repair motorways and are outside in all weather? If the point on danger and difficulty doesn't grab you, what about the mind numbing boredom generated by some jobs? Could you really be happy and fulfilled when you've just asked whether they want fries with that to the three hundredth person that day?

Teaching isn't that bad! Teaching is a job where we get paid a good wage to stand in a room and talk about things that interest us and attempt to impart our enthusiasm to others. We get to interact with people, we have some degree of autonomy and no two days are the same. Of course it is a little more complicated than that, and some positions are easier than others, but hopefully you get the point. Don't listen to the grumbling voices in the staffroom who try to convince you that the life of a teacher is the hardest life known to man. They don't really mean it – they are still in the job, after all!

2. It's not as easy as you think

On the other hand, the lot of the teacher is not as easy as some people think, and there's good reason to think that it has become significantly harder in recent years. It's quite infuriating to read articles or listen to phone-ins on education. Everyone has an opinion on how teachers should teach, how often work should be marked, what exams people should sit etc. There is a lack of respect for teachers' professional expertise. Someone once used the analogy of air travel. When we go on our holidays, we don't tell the pilot how to do his or her job; we respect the pilot's expertise. When we are having an operation, we don't give the surgeon advice on where to make the incision. Yet by and large the wider public don't always respect the expertise of the teacher. They went to school once, so of course they know how it should be done. However, for most right thinking adults, the experience of having a few children round to play or trying to organise games for a group of children full of food colouring at their son or daughter's birthday party brings the realisation that it might actually be quite difficult to be in charge of groups of children for several hours.

In addition the teacher's workload is unusual, and this is not always realised by those outside the profession. Yes, there are generous holidays, even if some of it is spent working, but evenings and weekends in term time are often filled in trying to make sure that everything gets done. Teachers don't necessarily work longer or shorter hours than anyone else, but the workload is compressed and intense. Surveys suggest a 55–60 hour working week for a teacher in term time is about the norm. If the job is that easy, why is it that half the people in Britain who are trained to teach no longer actually do so? We know that over 40% of newly qualified teachers do not make it to 5 years in the job. The amount of stress related illness and sick days in any school or college is often immense. What conclusions can we draw? Simply that the job is not easy, and not everyone can do it. Don't allow the uninformed outsider to put you down.

3. The struggle is mainly psychological

So how do we as teachers navigate this minefield? In recent years I have become convinced that the main battle that we face is actually psychological. The pressure on a teacher's mind is immense. Teachers face the battle in the classroom, where groups of students, each with their own issues, turn up in varying states, ranging from keen to learn to keen to make your life a misery. To do the job well takes a high degree of skill and energy. The demands of increased paperwork, challenging students and microscopic scrutiny of results bring their own pressures. Add to that the criticism of students, parents, managers and the media. There are an awful lot of negative inputs and experiences each day and it is easy for a teacher to end up agreeing that he or she is not up to the job. Yet each day in the classroom we are required to go on as a beacon of positivity and encouragement. The mismatch between what goes into our mind and how we have to perform is draining and cannot be sustained unless we find ways of dealing with these stresses. How we think about ourselves and our role as teachers is crucial in determining whether we survive and succeed in the job. Once we have sorted the psychological, we can begin to deal with the more practical strategies; this we will do in the latter parts of the book.

? Questions for reflection

1 If you weren't a teacher, what job would you do? Realistically would it match teaching for the daily variety, challenge and sense of fulfilment?

2 What things have you done as a teacher that you are proud of that you suspect some of your non-teacher friends would not have been able to do? Hold on to these thoughts.

Chapter 2

You are not alone – statistics and context

Some of the latest information on stress, workload, teacher retention etc. is shocking. The purpose of this chapter is to set a context and to raise awareness. We are not going to stay here and wallow, but it is important that we understand where we are if we are to have any hope of moving on. This chapter aims to address two seemingly simple questions: what is the current situation and what is causing it?

Some statistics and context

There have certainly been some eye catching and alarming statistics thrown around. Recently, the October 2015 YouGov survey carried out for the NUT claimed that 50% of teachers were planning to quit in the next two years. It certainly got people's attention. Of course there is often a grey area between a few thoughts about quitting and a definite intention – the questions were ambiguous. Equally there is a further gap between intention and action. As much as someone may intend to leave their position, the reality of mortgages and dependents may mean that they ultimately stay. All of this means that the number actually leaving is lower; however, if you think this might be a cause for celebration, then try asking yourself whether you want your own children taught by someone who is desperate to be elsewhere!

Stat attack

- Around 10% of UK teachers leave state sector teaching each year.
- 49,120 teachers left the state sector in 2014; this reduces to 35,980 if you remove the number of retirees.
- In 2011 37% of leavers were retirees. In 2014 this was 27%.
- If retirees are removed from the statistics, the number of leavers in 2014 is 9.2% of the workforce. It was 6.5% in 2010.
- Around half of those leaving teaching stay within the education sector in some form.

(Data taken from Worth, J, Bamford, S, and Durbin, B (2015) *Should I Stay or Should I Go?* NFER Analysis of Teachers Joining and Leaving the Profession. Slough: NFER.)

Even if the actual figures are significantly lower than the headlines, they are alarming enough. Around 40% of new teachers leave before the end of 5 years in the job and it is estimated that there are as many qualified teachers outside teaching as there are within. The increase in exits from the profession once the retirees are removed from the statistics is quite stark, and the NFER report suggests that although the current situation is stable, the impending surge in pupil numbers in secondary schools may expose a huge gap in the coming years. In fact, proportionally speaking, more secondary school teachers are leaving, and it is some secondary subjects that are under recruiting in terms of trainee numbers.

It's not about the money

'On average the wages of teachers that left for another job were 10% lower than those that stayed in teaching' (*Should I Stay or Should I Go*, p. 10). Despite the pay freeze that teachers have experienced in the last 5 years, which the teaching unions suggest amount to a 17% pay cut in real terms, we can in most cases rule out money as a factor in people leaving teaching. Bearing in mind the still relatively generous pension, the holidays and a higher than the national average salary, 35,000 leaving teaching each year is extraordinarily high.

Tired teachers – do they jump or are they pushed?

In her recent investigation for Schools Week, Laura McInerney identified the phenomenon of tired teachers. Whilst noting that there is an increasing number of young qualified teachers seeking work abroad, it may be that the 'tired teacher' goes some way to explaining the statistics. After all, around 50% of those leaving teaching tend to reappear in education in some form.

'Tired teachers manifest themselves in at least two forms. Firstly, there are those who become weary of the 50 hour+ working week treadmills and the heavy accountability regimes in their schools. They leave teaching or leave full time teaching and take part time or temporary contracts. They enjoy the teaching, they don't much care for everything else that comes with it and they want the freedom to move on if they so choose'(McInerney 2015).

Second there are tired teachers who have been deemed to be tired teachers by someone else. They are moved on from a school or college with a neutral reference; they may or may not go back into teaching and, if they do so, it is likely to be short term work or supply. In fact one senior union case worker I spoke to drew attention to the disproportionately high number of staff in their 50s who found themselves subject to capability proceedings. Whilst it is tempting to think that this is no great loss as these are likely to be our weakest teachers, it is worth bearing in mind that what makes good teaching can be quite subjective and that office politics can be quite powerful in some institutions.

What is troubling about both of our tired teacher sub-groups is that they are experienced. Rather than just losing teachers early in their careers who discover the job is not for them, or losing staff in their late 50s who retire early, we are starting to lose people mid-career.

Stress and workload

It is only relatively recently that any attempt at analysing why teachers leave and where they go has taken place. UKedchat conducted an online survey – stress scored highest. 'Internal politics (within school), bullying, and the work / life balance clash were also cited regularly from respondents' (Ukedchat 2014).

Most people, when they are being honest, recognise that teaching is a stressful job; it is regularly close to the top in lists of stressed professionals. Most people even understand that in term time teachers work phenomenally hard; only solicitors come close in terms of unpaid overtime. A 2014 ATL study reported that 80% of teachers surveyed felt stressed (the exact same percentage reported in a similar NASUWT survey in 2012) and that 55% believed that their job was having a negative effect on their health and wellbeing (Sellgren 2014).

In summary our problem seems to be one of significant numbers of teachers either leaving the profession, hovering around the edges of teaching as 'tired teachers', or hanging in there but becoming increasingly worried about their health and wellbeing as well as their ability to sustain their performance in the long term.

No wonder this is the case. The teachers' contract is notoriously open ended. It requires that teachers should work 1,265 hours as directed plus 'such reasonable additional hours as may be needed to enable the effective discharge of their professional duties.'

Given that there are constant changes to the understanding of what an effective discharge of professional duties is, it is hardly surprising that stress and tiredness are on the increase. You are not alone if you are tired, anxious and harbouring thoughts about whether there may be a better way of making ends meet.

So if you are currently in teaching, take a moment to congratulate yourself. Your resilience, particularly if you have done more than 5 years, is to be commended. Remember that the grass is not necessarily greener on the other side – there may or may not be less stress. It is more likely that there will be less pay. More importantly remember that things can and will change. Whether through the laws of supply and demand – or karma – the situation has to get better for teachers. It's worth hanging in there.

> **?** Questions for reflection
>
> 1 What is currently keeping you in teaching? Is it family respon-
>   sibilities, love of the job or something else?
> 2 You are likely to know some teachers who have quit. What
>   were their reasons? Did they jump or did they feel pushed?

Bibliography

McInerney, L (2015) *Why tired teachers might hold the clue to the teacher shortage.* Schools Week 26th November. Available from http://schoolsweek.co.uk/why-tired-teachers-might-hold-the-clue-to-the-teacher-shortage/?utm_content=buffer28131&utm_medium=social&utm_source=twitter.com&utm_campaign=buffer (Accessed 29th December 2015).

Sellgren, K (2014) *Teachers report rise in mental health fears.* BBC News Education. Available from http://www.bbc.co.uk/news/education-26990735 (Accessed 15th February 2016).

Ukedchat (2014) *UkEdMag: Careers when leaving teaching.* Ukedchat Website. Available from http://ukedchat.com/2014/02/17/ukedmag-careers-when-leaving-teaching/ (Accessed 29th December 2015).

Worth, J, Bamford, S, and Durbin, B (2015) *Should I Stay or Should I go?* NFER Analysis of Teachers Joining and Leaving the Profession. Slough: NFER.

Chapter 3

Stress – getting personal

I became a ghost of my former self. When I've not been working, I've been thinking about work. Even holidays have been at least partly dominated by my working life. Perhaps this is partly a personal deficiency in me but also a true reflection of the demands of teaching in the UK today . . . Working 50, 60, 70 hours a week means that some of my great educational heroes have become foreigners to their own children . . . We really are entering educational death row. Human bodies cannot sustain the impact of this job in its current form. The evidence is there for all to see.

(Former History Teacher Thomas Rogers 2015)

Behind the statistics outlined in the previous chapter of teachers leaving the profession and those who were staying but at a cost to their health and wellbeing are many personal stories. They are often stories like the one above. In researching and acquiring data for this book, through conversations with friends and colleagues, many similar stories emerged. And sadly I wasn't looking particularly hard. The aim of this chapter is to look at what exactly we mean by stress and consider where exactly we might be on the continuum between healthy and stressed out. Before we do that, however, it is necessary to look at the thing that is commonly believed to be the number one cause of stress: workload.

The workload challenge

Every three years the UK government conducts a survey of teachers and asks them to submit a workload diary. The most recent survey was carried out in 2013 and, following a little bit of gentle persuasion on social media, the results were eventually published a year or so later.

Role/Sector	Hours worked each week	Classroom teaching hours	% Time spent working out of hours*
Classroom Teachers (Primary)	59.3	19	23.8%
Classroom Teachers (Secondary)	55.7	19.6	21.4%
Classroom Teachers (Academy)	55.2	20.2	19.7%
Headteachers (Secondary)	63.3	2.8	21.5%

* Out of hours was defined as before 8 a.m., after 6 p.m. and on weekends.
Adapted from DFE Teacher workload diary survey (2013).

This suggests that, for most classroom teachers, only around one third of their working hours are spent in the classroom. All types of teachers surveyed were doing well over 10 hours per week 'out of hours', and 44% of those surveyed believed that there had been an increase in the amount of unnecessary administrative tasks in the past couple of years.

In 2015 the government bravely set up the workload challenge. They invited teachers to describe what was frustrating them about their workload and suggest ways that things could be better. They received over 48,000 responses. Amongst the key concerns were:

- Marking and feedback – Specifically, unrealistic expectations as to frequency of marking and depth of comments. A primary school teacher could be expected to mark 90–120 books per day (one per subject per child for each session he/she had taught); a secondary school teacher may be required up to 300 books per fortnight (based on a 2-week timetable with 10 classes). Some schools had adopted a policy of requiring students to respond to feedback and for the teacher to mark again. This was being audited by senior managers.

- Planning and observation documentation – A requirement to plan on a specific proforma and submit detailed plans for weekly scrutiny. This would be further complicated for lesson observations.
- Data entry and analysis – The routine copying and pasting of information and the request to submit data on performance of individual classes on a regular basis.
- Constant monitoring and accountability structures – One example cited was performance management systems, but what comes across strongly from all responses was a frustration at a lack of trust.
- Constant change – In terms of Ofsted requirements, exam board specifications, assessment procedures, league table measures etc.

Add to that the requirement to answer emails, maintain the VLE, contact parents and other significant agencies, logging of incidents, following up poor behaviour, attending meetings, writing ILPs and undertaking CPD. A teacher's workload can easily become a bottomless pit, and a sense of not having done everything – and that it is impossible to have done everything – is surely one of the causes of teacher stress.

> Stress is 'a process that can occur when there is a mismatch between perceived pressures of the work situation and the individual's ability to cope with it' (Education Service Advisory Committee 1990).

"I'm fine. Thanks for asking."

When asked how we are, it is easy to reply that we are fine. To give a brief analogy with physical health, although I am broadly fine, I am aware that I have a slight crick in my neck from having slept awkwardly last night and the occasional cough from last month's cold. If I had to give my physical health at this moment as a percentage, I might say I was 90% well.

Just as our physical health fluctuates daily (hourly?) and it would be a clumsy overgeneralisation to have two groups of people, the healthy and the sick; so too our mental and emotional wellbeing is on a similar continuum. We are all somewhere on the continuum. Just as physically there are occasions when we recognise that our condition needs expert help and a doctor is the only answer, the same principle extends to our mental and emotional wellbeing. If your percentage is that low, then it is vital for your sake, those around you and the students you teach that you get the help that you need.

However, assuming that you are at least slighter better than that, there is of course that middle range of illnesses where we are able to self-diagnose what is wrong and nip off to the nearest supermarket for something to alleviate the symptoms. The rest of this chapter – and indeed the book – aims to address the middle ground: the moderately stressed.

Am I stressed?

There are a number of factors that may indicate stress. Some of the categories below overlap, but if you suffer from several of these, one possible explanation could be stress:

Physical – There are a number of physical indicators of stress, including tension headaches, muscle aching, tiredness, sleep problems, and a tendency to catch regular colds.

Mental/emotional – [What I notice about my thoughts and feelings.] Common indicators are feelings of anxiety/worry, memory loss, guilt, anger, feelings of resentment, a sense of isolation, a loss of self-esteem, feelings of failure or helplessness, indecisiveness, difficulties with concentration.

Behavioural – [What I (and others) notice about my actions.] Aggression, over reaction to minor difficulties, loss of libido, crying/other extremes of emotion, being over sensitive, passivity/indifference to danger,[1] change in eating patterns, increased consumption of alcohol/nicotine/caffeine, becoming accident prone and distracted, becoming withdrawn.

We all benefit from a little stress. If we have no stress, then we become bored and less productive. However, if we are over stressed we can become tired and exhausted and our performance declines. The list above may make for an interesting self-assessment, but one point worth noting is that often it is those who are close to us that spot the signs first. We can very often be to slow to spot what is obvious in our thoughts and behaviour. It is well worth sharing the list with a close colleague at work or trusted family member and asking them to watch your back. Also it is worth reflecting on times when you have been stressed – what were the triggers? Which straw broke the camel's back? What can you learn for the future?

? Questions for reflection

1   How do you feel when you read accounts like that of Tom Rogers? Hopefully you have not reached that point, but what aspects of his experience do you identify with?

2   Roughly where would you place yourself on the mentally healthy/stressed continuum? What are signs that you notice when you are becoming more stressed?

3   Who is your trusted friend who will look out for you and talk sense into you? How can you develop such a relationship, in which you watch each other's backs, as it were?

Note

1   My wife and I experienced this when our son was born prematurely and spent 12 weeks seriously ill on a ventilator. Everyday tasks such as crossing the road became difficult due to poor concentration and seemed too trivial to think about! I have spoken to a couple of colleagues who have reported similar indifference to danger whilst stressed at work. One commented that he became more prone to pull out at a junction!

Bibliography

DFE (Department for Education) (2013) *Teacher workload diary survey 2013*. TNS BMRB. Available from https://www.gov.uk/government/uploads/system/uploads/attachment_data/file/285941/DFE-RR316.pdf (Accessed 30th December 2015).

Education Service Advisory Committee of the Health and Safety Committee (1990) *Managing Occupational Stress: A Guide for Managers and Teachers in the School Sector.* London: HMSO.

Gibson, S, Oliver, L, and Dennison, M (2015) *Workload challenge: Analysis of teacher consultation responses.* CooperGibson Research. Available from http://www.coopergibson.co.uk/RR445_-_Workload_Challenge_-_Analysis_of_teacher_consultation_responses_FINAL.pdf (Accessed 6th April 2016).

Rogers, T (2015) *We are entering educational death row: Human bodies cannot sustain the impact of teaching in its current form.* TES (15th December 2015). Available from https://www.tes.com/news/school-news/breaking-views/we-are-entering-educational-death-row-human-bodies-cannot-sustain (Accessed 30th December 2015).

Part 1

The mind of the teacher

Chapter 4

Psychology of teachers – knowing the traps

Although an optimum amount of stress is helpful and can even improve our productivity, it is clear that the situation for many teachers is one of too much stress to the extent that, finding their workload overwhelming, they are becoming burned out and leaving. Explanations of how people become stressed typically involve three elements or steps:

1   The facts of a situation, including what we have/haven't done, what we have been asked to do, student grades etc.

2   A judgement about our competence and success regarding the above; this is our own judgement, but it may be reinforced by what others say or do.

3   Thoughts, reactions and behaviour based on the judgement.

Given that we cannot always control some of the things that are happening at stage 1, we need to try to understand some of the things that are taking place in teachers' minds. Understanding why we think a certain way is the first step to trying to change it. This chapter will look at theories about how the mind works and then focus on some of the peculiarities of the minds of teachers.

Philosophy corner – from Aristotle to the chimp

As far back as Plato and Aristotle, philosophers have puzzled over the nature of the mind – in particular, the inner conflict between the rational and the emotional. Plato believed that the emotions were not that important; they were like a wayward horse that the charioteer had to bring into line. The soul and its logic was the charioteer. Unfortunately, we cannot separate body and mind quite as easily as Plato suggests. We are a little more complicated than that.

More helpful to our understanding was the work of Aristotle, who believed that both the rational and irrational aspects of the mind were part of who we are. Crucial to our success in life was the development of our virtues; this meant managing our emotions. It is appropriate that Daniel Goleman begins his much acclaimed book on *Emotional Intelligence* (1995) with a chapter on Aristotle. It is Goleman's view that emotional intelligence – the ability to be aware of the emotions of ourselves and others and to use this information to guide behaviour – is more important to an individual's success than their IQ.

The insight that the emotional aspect of our psychology is important and is more immediate is developed in a slightly more accessible form by the sports psychologist Steve Peters (2011) in his book *The Chimp Paradox*. Peters contrasts the basic limbic component of the brain (the chimp) with the frontal (the human). The chimp's 'thinking' is quick and based on feelings and impressions; this is not dissimilar to what Goleman calls 'quick and sloppy' emotional thinking. According to Peters, being aware of our emotional aspect, our inner chimp, means being aware that there is an aspect of us that is irrational. It jumps to opinions, is guilty of black and white thinking, is paranoid, and catastrophises situations.

Scenario

John has never quite clicked with the deputy head. This means he can have involuntary negative emotions when she is around. Following a brief conversation in the corridor about a student, the deputy head remarks, 'You clearly have the student's best interests at heart.' The chimp/irrational side of his brain springs to life. 'Does she mean I am a soft touch? Does she mean that I don't have the school's interests at heart? There are likely to be redundancies this year, and perhaps she is formulating a case against me.' All of this in the first couple of seconds, before the more rational side has chance to reflect.

Say what you see

Just as our eyes can be drawn to some things and not others (gestalt is the technical term) so too our minds can fall into ways of interpreting past events. Some thoughts suck us in – they engage us on an emotional level. We keep playing them over and over like a favourite CD regardless of whether they are helpful or accurate. In his recent book, *You Are Not So Smart*, David McRaney (2011) argues that our memories actually reconstruct rather than replay events. In fact the events that we think about most often are probably least accurately remembered – our mind puts its own spin on things! Perhaps that lesson from yesterday that you can't stop thinking about wasn't as bad as you think. The point is that sometimes we have to challenge our thoughts rather than just accepting them. There is nothing to be gained from dwelling on unhelpful thoughts. If we know that a certain train goes to the place we least want to go, we don't get on that train. Yet so often we get on trains of thinking that lead us to destinations of feelings and behaviour that are not helpful to us.

The mind of the teacher

As well as the above, there are a number of peculiarities to the teacher's situation. Let's consider the type of people who tend to become teachers and the situations they find once they are qualified. At the risk of generalising, teachers are:

1   Achievers – Teachers have generally been successful in education and are used to doing well. They are not used to failing. When, as teachers, we find something difficult or we make a mess of something, it is especially difficult for us to deal with as we are not used to it. More of this when we consider mindsets (chapter 29).

2   Carers – Most of us came into the job because we wanted to make a difference. We actually like young people most days and want them to do well. The danger is that we can care too much. It is a well attested phenomenon that those in caring positions can become in greater need of care themselves. Yet who counsels the counsellor? By our own nature and that of the job, we find it very hard to step back and let go.

3   Perfectionists – We are perfectionists who aim to please others. This has been reinforced during our time at school. We worked hard, our teachers praised us, and on the occasions where our work needed improvement, we took the criticisms to heart and made sure we did something about it. Even now when we are observed and five positive things are said with one negative, which do we remember? This perfectionism is a common factor in most teachers and particularly in those who have experienced mental health issues. Others may give us a hard time, but that pales into insignificance compared to the hard time that some of us give ourselves.

4   Isolated – Although to some extent a school or college is a team, when we step into a classroom we work for much of the day in isolation. We are the only adult in the room. This leads to two issues: first, we have less of the peer support and encouragement you might receive in other jobs, which is why it is so important to get to the staffroom at lunch and break; second, it can be harder to get a sense of how well we are doing. We don't often see others teaching and it is easy for us in our silo to conclude that what is happening in other people's classrooms is far better than what is happening in our own. One of the unfortunate side effects of league tables and PSP is that we are forced to compete with each other, and this merely adds to the isolation.

5   On a Rollercoaster – A day in teaching contains hundreds of interactions. A child misbehaving, a student in tears because of events at home, another student who still doesn't get an equation despite three explanations, another is 5 minutes late again, another is quiet and subdued – all in lesson 1, and there are 4 more lessons to go. There are interactions with staff, angry parents and the 30 emails that arrived during the day whilst you were teaching. All these interactions engage us to some degree on an emotional level; it may not even be conscious. A day in teaching is a mental rollercoaster, and it can take its toll.

Teaching is a job that demands our emotional investment and energy. It is a psychological process as much as a physical one in the classroom. We ignore the psychological aspects of the job at our peril.

Yes, but how? Practically speaking

Pause. Don't act when overly emotional. Step away from the PC and don't send the email. Don't tell the student (or the deputy head) exactly what you think!

When you are feeling negative, seek company; it overcomes the isolation, and you can test your feelings with a friend or colleague. Maybe the situation is not as bad as it seems.

? Questions for reflection

1 What is the main weapon that your chimp uses against you? Is it anger, guilt or feelings of inferiority?

2 Are things really as bad as you thought? Talk a difficult situation over with a friend. Is it really as hopeless as you think?

Bibliography

Goleman, D (1995) *Emotional Intelligence – Why It Can Matter More Than IQ,* New York: Bloomsbury.

McRaney, D (2011) *You Are Not So Smart,* New York: Gotham Books/Penguin Group.

Peters, S (2011) *The Chimp Paradox,* London: Vermilion.

Chapter 5

Guilt

I shouldn't be writing this. I should be preparing tomorrow's lessons and, although they are by and large prepared already, I should probably have an extra task to support the less able. I should ring the associate teacher to arrange the teaching practice. I should review the target grades of my classes, I should edit the open evening PowerPoint, I should be more organised with my photocopying, I should respond to those emails, I should ring that parent. I should spend more time with my own children.

As teachers we are at the mercy of the 'should' monster. Whenever we do a task, it appears to remind us of a completely different task. When we decide to take time off, it looms even larger in the form of a fully fledged list of things and deadlines. The longer I do this job, the more I am convinced that for whatever reason, we are as a profession strangely more prone to guilt than most. This chapter looks at why we feel so guilty and questions how logical all of this guilt actually is.

Where does this all come from?

In everyday life we associate guilt with breaking a legal or moral standard. So if we were to kick a student (it's just an example!), we would be guilty both in law and in a moral sense. If we were to tell a lie, there may be no legal guilt, yet we might view ourselves as morally guilty. However, the guilt we feel as teachers is neither of these. It is essentially a subjective thing; we perceive ourselves to have failed to live up to our own very high standards of conduct and excellence.

So, for example, if we have an expectation either from managers or from our own sense of standards that we ought to always mark work and hand it back at the next lesson, then when we are unable to do that, we feel guilty. That is one of the main reasons we feel guilty so often. This is not helped by the conversation on INSET days. We listen to colleagues describing what goes on in their lessons, the sharing of good practice. As we listen to colleagues describing their lessons, we are aware that we just don't match up. Of course that isn't the effect that managers or the colleagues sharing intend. They really are trying to help, but teachers' minds are strange things!

Sometimes I wonder how accurate and honest their descriptions are. Are they really that good all the time? Somehow I doubt it. Nevertheless, in addition to our own expectation, there develops almost a peer pressure that ramps up the expectations. We become all too aware of our own limitations in comparison – more guilt. Clearly this is not psychologically healthy. What, if anything, can be done?

Philosophy corner: 'Ought implies can'

As an RS & Philosophy teacher, I am aware that the ethics of Immanuel Kant is often one of the driest parts of the specification for students. Little do they realise that he has an idea that can solve teachers' problems (and anyone else's!). The key phrase is 'ought implies can'.

Kant was interested in moral responsibility: what exactly is a person's duty? First, consider the following two sentences: 'You ought to buy your wife flowers' and 'You ought to be 6 inches taller'. There is a difference between these two imperatives. The second one is not within my power. This essentially is Kant's point. You can only really use the word 'ought' with its implications of duty and responsibility if it is something that can actually be done. To say that you ought to help an old lady cross the road is reasonable if you are within the vicinity of the road. To say that you ought to stop all the world's wars before nightfall is not. (Unless you are a world leader and you're having a really good day.)

Being logical about guilt

So how does this help teachers who, as we have already said, are particularly prone to guilt? We feel responsible for everything. We agonise over the best way to teach a lesson, worry over the detail or lack of it in our marking, fret over students who may fail exams, and so on. I'm not suggesting that we shouldn't take these things seriously, but I am suggesting that we should stop beating ourselves up. Remember 'Ought implies can'! We can only do what we can do. Here are three ways this might apply.

1 Things that are logically impossible

Imagine someone suggests that you ought to make 2 + 2 add up to 5. Clearly you can't. To be fair most of the things we are asked to do as teachers are not impossible. They actually can be done. However, often in doing one thing we end up neglecting another. Sometimes instructions are contradictory and pull in different directions. We are encouraged to allow weaker students onto academic A Level courses, for instance, yet are told to improve results. We are encouraged to adapt to students' learning styles and also to prepare them for adult life. I've worked in various places and never once has my boss asked me what my preferred working style is so that he/she can adapt to my needs. Even though the 'oughts' may be worthwhile in themselves, they pull against each other and we cannot logically do all of them, all of the time.

2 Things that depend on others

Suppose we are told that we ought to improve the pass rate for the course we're teaching. Absolutely, we want to do this, and we will work our hardest to achieve it. But it doesn't just depend on us. If a student cannot get up in a morning, is hospitalised for weeks or discovers that the delights of the party scene hold more attractions than A Levels, then that's down to them not us. Here's the strange thing. In order to hold us responsible for something such as results, we have to be free to make genuine choices about what we do, how we teach, our methods, materials etc. The idea of responsibility implies that I am a free and autonomous person. However, if we hold the teacher solely responsible for results, then we are denying our students responsibility and ultimately their status as persons. We are saying that they are just objects that behave in predictable ways in response to our teaching. However, they're not. Students make their own choices, and sometimes we cannot wave a magic wand no matter how much we would wish to. The same applies to our senior managers; decisions they make will affect what we can or can't do. We have all had experiences no doubt of being directed to do something that we are certain will be detrimental to outcomes.

3 Things, things and more things

To be fair most of the things we are asked to do, we can actually do. They are reasonable. Sometimes the main problem is the volume of things; we cannot do all things well. As one of the respondents in the workload challenge stated, the issue is the 'aggregate of things.' Of the 10 perfectly reasonable balls we are asked to juggle, maybe eight are in the air, a ninth one is falling and a tenth one is smashed on the floor, and we hope to clear it up later before anyone notices. Here lies perhaps our biggest battle with guilt. We can teach good lessons to all our groups tomorrow, mark the two sets of essays, and finish the reports, but can we manage to do all three well? If we do, the teaching guilt goes, but we start to feel that we are neglecting our family. 'I ought to spend more time with the children' and 'I could do with a decent night's sleep.' How to balance all these commitments is a real challenge. 'Ought implies can'. We can only do what we can do; we are only responsible for that which is possible. Can anyone else really do any better? Maybe a single celibate monk who doesn't need a lot of sleep, but I suspect his lessons wouldn't be as interesting as ours.

Guilt is a natural emotion that we feel because we care deeply about doing a good job. However, it is important that we remember that our brain is not always totally logical. You are only allowed to feel guilty if you could genuinely have done differently with the time and resources at your disposal. And even if you could have done better, learning from the situation rather than wallowing in guilt is a better reaction.

? **Questions for reflection**

1 What things do you feel most guilty about as a teacher? Are they things that are within your control?

2 If you were to address the things you currently feel guilty about, what other things would you have to drop? Which are more important?

Chapter 6

Anxiety and fear

Our profession has lost the status it once had and our judgements in the classroom day to day are checked and scrutinised as never before. If you work as a teacher or in education you will know that there is no balance. In term time we are buried with work with maybe half a weekend off in a week – if we're lucky. Holidays are more of a recovery period. We discuss progress not in terms of 'So-and-so learnt to do this today!' but, 'Have they made the required progress so I will meet my performance targets?' At the moment I feel constantly stressed and tired. I tend to go to bed worrying about school and waking up still worrying about something to do with school. I will be looking to leave full time teaching. This is both exciting and nerve-wracking, but ultimately I know that this is the right choice for me.

(Anonymous secondary school teacher,
Ukedchat 2014)

We are losing many of our better teachers. They are teachers who do not necessarily want to go; at least in terms of their salary, they do not necessarily have anything better to go to. We are losing them to fear and anxiety. They are worrying themselves sick, quite literally. This chapter will look at some of the roots of teacher anxiety and consider what we can do to relieve the situation.

Roots of fear

It is normal in all walks of life to have some anxiety over our work; it shows we care. As teachers, we have so many things to care or worry about. Amongst these, and in no particular order, are:

- Getting everything done – planning, marking, administration.
- Judgements and reviews – lesson observations, performance management.
- Student progress – or lack of it. Can I prove they have progressed? What if some haven't?
- Challenging behaviour – students and sometimes their parents.

Add to that our own natural insecurities, and we have a recipe for anxiety. During a conversation with an exam board colleague who had risen to a relatively senior position within his school, he admitted to me that he faced each academic year worrying that this was the year that 'they were going to find him out'. I wonder how many of us as teachers suffer from 'imposter syndrome'?

Psychology corner: Maslow's hierarchy of needs

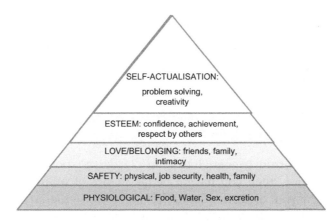

Diagram 6.1 Abraham Maslow's Hierarchy of Needs (adapted by the author from Maslow, 1970)

The psychologist Abraham Maslow developed his theory of the hierarchy of needs. Maslow argues that the layers on Diagram 6.1 are different levels of need; they determine what motivates us. We can only move on, as it were, once the needs on a certain level have been met.

So, for instance, we will not feel motivated to be creative in our planning if lower-level needs have not been met; for example, if we fear for our job security or we have had only 6 hours sleep.

Applying Maslow's idea to modern education systems is quite enlightening. It becomes easy to see how we have arrived at our present state. We need to feel safe and valued by others around us. Yet everything in modern education seems to operate against that. Whilst it was wrong to effectively allow weaker teachers a job for life, we have replaced this with a volatile system where you are only as good as your last results or observation and pay progression is not guaranteed. Staff do not necessarily feel safe and younger staff particularly worry about how to pay their bills. Observation, both formal and informal, has been a mixed blessing. As we rightly open the door to allow feedback, we are opening it to criticism that can knock confidence.

We have built schools and colleges based on the principle of fear. But the more that people neglect their physical and emotional needs, the less they feel secure in their jobs, and the more likely it is that the quality of teaching and education will actually go down. As John Tomsett puts it in his excellent recent book, *This Much I Know about Love Over Fear*, 'the one thing that destroys the energy of a workplace culture is a climate of fear. Conversely, people's energies are maximised when they feel loved and safe. Love wins over fear every time' (Tomsett 2015, p. 89).

Leadership byte

If you are fortunate enough to be in a leadership position in your organisation, then you have a better chance of influencing the culture of your organisation. Reflect on Maslow's hierarchy: How safe do staff feel? Do they fear for their jobs? Do they know how well they are doing? Do they feel respected and valued? Does their workload regularly cause them to neglect their family or to lose sleep? Is staff turnover high? Are the right people leaving and for the right reasons?

What can you influence in your position to make things better?

Dealing with anxiety

First, do not worry. Obviously, that is easier said than done, but where possible try your best not to worry. Remember that your inner chimp is a catastrophiser who will always present you with the worst case scenario. Worry doesn't solve anything and, in fact, just gives you something extra to do. It saps your mental energy.

One way of doing this may be to ask yourself the question, 'What is in my control?' Try writing down the things that are making you anxious. Divide them into three categories: things you control, things you can influence in some way, and things you have no control over whatsoever. Although it is hard to do, there is no point worrying over the final category even if someone else expects you to worry about it. For example in colleges we are measured on retention – the number of students who complete the course – and last year students left my courses because of a range of things outside my control, including cancer diagnosis, domestic violence and abuse at home. Tragic, but nothing that I could do would have prevented them from leaving.

Yes, but how? Practically speaking

Recognising that the above is challenging and may sound like a meaningless platitude, consider also the following practical steps:

1   Don't neglect the physical. Try to get 8 hours sleep each night; situations often do appear different in the morning after you have rested. Don't miss meals. (See later sections on energy.)

2   Connect with others. Whether they be friends or family, aim to spend time with others. Not only does this meet a key psychological need and ensure that you have one less thing to feel bad about, distraction is also a key weapon against anxiety. Ensure that your mind has other things to focus on.

3   Get organised and plan ahead. Alleviate the fear of your large impending workload by planning ahead and getting organised. What will you do and by when? More on this in chapters 32–34.

Doing it for the kids

Given that as teachers we frequently put our own needs aside in order to prioritise our students, I leave this until last. We need to put our wellbeing higher up on our list precisely because of our students.

Natasha Devon, the former Department for Education mental health champion, writing in the TES, states, 'To improve the mental health of young people we should start by tackling stress amongst teachers.' She goes on to argue that 'There is no doubt in my mind that teachers are fast becoming the primary mental health-care giver to an entire generation of children and adolescents. But who will look after them?' (Devon 2015). Students learn from who we are, not just what we say and do. We have to be careful not to transmit our stress and anxiety to students.

Yet it is not just about student mental health; there is some evidence that teacher wellbeing can have positive effects on results too. The 2014 report, 'Healthy Teachers, Higher Marks', commissioned by the Teacher Support Network, whilst being honest in admitting that there were many variables at work, suggested that '8% of variance in SATs results can be attributed to teacher wellbeing' (Bajorek, Gulliford and Taskila 2014, p. 11). All of which suggests we must do all we can to reduce our anxiety levels.

?   **Questions for reflection**

1   Do you worry about things on the lower sections of Maslow's hierarchy (Diagram 6.1), such as job security? What, if anything, can you do to change the situation?

2   List some of the things you worry about in relation to your job. Are there things on the list that you cannot change at all?

3   Honestly, do you sometimes add to your own worries by being disorganised? What could you do better? Read chapters 32–34 or talk to an organised colleague that you admire.

Bibliography

Bajorek, Z, Gulliford, J, and Taskila, T (2014) *Healthy teachers, higher marks? Establishing a link between teacher health & wellbeing and student outcomes.* The work foundation and the Teacher Support Network. Available from http://www.theworkfoundation.com/DownloadPublication/Report/369_TSN%20REPORT%20FINAL%20AUGUST%201%202014.pdf (Accessed 6th April 2016).

Devon, N (2015) *To improve the mental health of young people, we should start by tackling stress among teachers.* TES (23rd November 2015). Available from https://www.tes.com/news/school-news/breaking-views/improve-mental-health-young-people-we-should-start-tackling-stress (Accessed 5th March 2016).

Maslow, AH (1970) *Motivation and Personality.* New York: Harper & Row.

Peters, S (2011) *The Chimp Paradox,* London: Vermilion.

Tomsett, J (2015) *This Much I Know about Love Over Fear,* Camarthen: Crown House.

Ukedchat (2014) *UkEdMag: Careers when leaving teaching.* Ukedchat Website. Available from http://ukedchat.com/2014/02/17/ukedmag-careers-when-leaving-teaching/ (Accessed 29th December 2015).

Chapter 7

Anger and frustration

My teacher training course was of little help in preparing me to manage actual classes and deal with the sheer frustration I would feel as a result of my inability to do so. After a couple of teaching practices and a maternity cover in generally pleasant schools where I occasionally raised my voice if needed and it worked, I arrived in my first permanent post in a high school in more challenging circumstances. Here my one behaviour management strategy of shouting and sending students out of the room was exposed. The sight of me losing my cool was no doubt a great entertainment to the students who didn't actually want to be in the room in the first place and, if sent out, could create further disruption by face pulling through the window.

Following one particularly shambolic lesson with a year 10 group – several students had been given detentions and been sent out and others had been rude and unpleasant – my anger reached such a point that once the group had exited the room, I proceeded to kick the living daylights out of a metal filing cabinet. For the record it is never a smart move to pick a fight with a metal filing cabinet; even now, when I have been standing for long periods, I feel a slight twinge in my right foot.

Over the next 5 or so years I slowly by trial and error figured out some of the basics of classroom management. Emotionally, having rationalised guilt and anxiety to some extent, anger and frustration were my Achilles heel. This chapter looks at what the triggers are for anger as well as considering some of the ways we might overcome it.

Types of anger

> Anyone can become angry – that is easy. But to be angry with the right
> person, to the right degree, at the right time, for the right purpose, and
> in the right way – this is not easy.
>
> Aristotle, *The Nichomachean Ethics* (1959)

Not all anger is necessarily a bad thing; there are different types of
anger that we need to harness. There is the feigned or pretend anger
that we should have when we reprimand a student. Learn from my
mistakes; using real anger takes too much energy! There is the righ-
teous anger that responds to injustices such as bullying or poor treatment of a student or colleague. These are legitimate and generally
healthy. But there is also a different type of anger . . .

It really winds me up . . .

There are a number of things that can raise our blood pressure and
wind us up in the course of our working day:

- Students – obviously. Teaching can be a frustrating business. We
  work incredibly hard to give each of our students the opportunity
  to reach their potential. Yet so often it seems that just as we have
  begun to sail the ship of learning towards its destination, several
  of our passengers have thrown themselves overboard.
- Sudden changes to plans, whether this is an additional task, a
  moving deadline or something that has not been communicated
  to you. You had sorted out your week and then someone bowls you
  a curve ball.
- Being badly treated or judged adversely. The observer just didn't
  see the lesson as you did. The headteacher has promoted someone
  else. You have been unfairly criticised.

Identity and control freakery

As teachers we are more prone than most to developing control freak-
ery. Indeed we are asked to manage learning – we have to exert some

form of control. Unfortunately we are dealing with people, and people do not always behave in the ways we expect, they do not always do what is best for them and, despite our best efforts to steer them to safety, they are prone to lemming like dives from cliffs. To make matters worse, along comes a senior manager to ask you what more you could have done to help.

As with fear and anxiety, anger can be linked to control. It is a frustration at not having control over things that you want to control. Something (or quite often someone) is standing between you and the goal that you have set out to achieve. Anger is often about having goals blocked. Education requires that we set ambitious targets. Then things get in our way – students, managers etc. Sometimes the goals are changed mid game as governments decide to exchange one way of doing things or measuring us for another. This can feel like an attack on who we are as well as what we are trying to achieve. If they don't behave or achieve in my class, I am not the good teacher that I thought I was.

Remember the chimp

> You are not responsible for the nature of your Chimp but you are responsible for managing it.
>
> (Peters 2011, p. 11)

In *The Chimp Paradox* (2011), Dr Steve Peters gives the analogy of the emotional side of the brain being like a chimp that you, the human, has to manage. These insights are particularly pertinent when it comes to anger. Your anger is a natural part of you; it may even be justified, although it is wise to be mindful of your 'chimp's' tendency to take things personally that were not intended that way. Peters suggests a two stage strategy that you can use to help manage your chimp. The two stages are relevant to managing anger but can be applied to a number of emotional states:

1   Exercising the Chimp – In a safe place allow your 'chimp' to let off steam either by writing down exactly why you feel angry or by

ranting to a trusted friend or colleague. Once the emotion has been vented, as it were, you are ready to think more rationally.

2   Boxing the Chimp – After exercise we are able to reason with our chimp. We may concede that our marking has been misjudged as poor or that we have been wrongly denied a pay rise; the emotions we feel are not wrong, but we are deciding rationally not to take things further. It is about understanding how your chimp acts and being aware that in a sense it is not you; it is stronger than you.

Yes, but how? Practically speaking

As well as exercising and boxing our chimps, there are other practical things that we can do when we are feeling frustrated and angry about things at work:

1   As with other emotions, distraction can work wonders. Do something else, such as reading a chapter of a book or listening to music. Go to the staffroom and grab a cup of tea.

2   Don't go to bed angry – and if possible don't leave work angry. We may have been to a wedding where the Biblical advice of not going to bed angry has been given. It's good advice. It is also good where possible to avoid leaving work angry. At the school I mentioned at the start of the chapter, a small group of staff would gather in the staffroom at around 4:30 p.m. after detentions to have a cuppa and a laugh about the day. These informal therapy sessions were vital in ensuring that people were themselves by the time they got home.

3   Conversely, sometimes it is good to leave promptly after 'one of those days' provided you are not in an agitated and emotional state by the time you get home.

   Finally, given that very often anger and frustration are the result of blocked goals, it may be worth adjusting some of your goals to more realistic ones. Sometimes we need to accept those things that we cannot change and realise that setbacks or failures do not threaten our long term identity as a teacher.

Questions for reflection

1 When (notice not 'if') you have lost it with staff or students, what were the triggers? What were you trying to control or trying to be? What goals were blocked?

2 What diffuses your anger? Could you have a certain CD in your car, a book or some chocolate in your locker for when you've had one of those days?

3 Which of your goals are unrealistic? How can you balance the high expectations of yourself and others with a little realism?

Bibliography

Aristotle (1959) *The Nichomachean Ethics*. London: Oxford University Press.
Peters, S (2011) *The Chimp Paradox*, London: Vermilion.

Chapter 8

Depression and reaching rock bottom

I knew that review meetings could be tough, but this was something else. We had for the first time in over 10 years achieved poor results on one of our courses. Sitting before me were two senior managers, a governor and an external consultant. I tried to explain why in my view the previous year's results were anomalous. It didn't go down well; I was informed that this sounded like complacency. I was reminded that I was being paid generously to manage the department and that an unqualified teacher (employed as a learning mentor) seemed to be having more impact than me. As I tried politely as I could to answer each of their questions, I was interrupted. I left the meeting in no doubt that I was not up to scratch. The next day I received the report from the consultant's monitoring visit. His verbal feedback had been mixed: hard but fair. The written version had only the negatives.

That evening and the weekend that followed it was one of the most challenging points mentally in my career. I attended an event at my son's school in the evening but I wasn't really there. Phrases from the review meeting kept coming back to me. I struggled with sleep that weekend and, following a few conversations with my wonderful wife, agreed that if I felt no better on Monday morning I would go to the doctor. I did feel a little better on Monday morning and battled through the rest of the year. Mentally there were a lot of ups and downs. Looking back I was probably at least borderline depressed for some of that year; with hindsight maybe I should have taken some time off. This chapter is about depression and hitting rock bottom more generally. Just how do you know when enough is enough?

Circumstances and events – when life affects work

Of course not all our reasons for reaching rock bottom may be school related. As teachers we are not immune from the big traumas of life: bereavement, serious illness and relationship breakdown, to name just three. Unfortunately teaching is not the sort of job where we can stroll in, meander through the day doing the bare minimum and go home, only giving work a thought as we drive in the next day. Teaching demands that you give of yourself, are mentally sharp and are on the ball in the classroom. We may just about be able to handle teaching, but then life sends us a curveball.

Early on in my teaching career, my wife and I had our first child, born prematurely at 28 weeks and weighing 1.5 pounds. Although he was on an incubator and at times critically ill, I returned to work after a few days. Big mistake! The students sensed weakness and classroom management actually became harder. After a few days at the end of a particularly difficult Tuesday afternoon with the worst year 10 group in school, I walked into the head's office shaking and announced that I needed to take time out. The school was great and I returned two weeks later to find that all the things I hadn't done no longer needed doing.

Key message

No one is indispensable to any organisation – as much as it may hurt us to say it. If there are extreme circumstances outside of work that are affecting you, speak up. Make sure your line manager and your headteacher know. Ask to take time off if you need it. Most (but not all) institutions are more supportive than you think.

Circumstances and events – when work affects life

Unfortunately too often for teachers it is the other way round. As in the story I opened the chapter with, difficult events at work have a severely detrimental effect on life outside work. Because of the nature of the job, there is always going to be some blurring of the lines between work and home. If you do feel at rock bottom, try asking yourself these questions:

- Am I overly short tempered? Am I overly emotional in other ways, such as bursting into tears frequently?
- Is my thinking almost exclusively pessimistic? Am I catastrophising?
- Am I tired or lethargic?
- Have I lost interest in things outside of work? How healthy are my significant relationships (e.g. my marriage)?
- Am I mentally absent despite being physically present in the room?

Obviously I have to make the disclaimer that I am not a doctor of either the body or the mind. **If in any doubt, seek professional help.** As with many of these checklists, it may be worth asking the opinion of a close relative or friend who has your best interests at heart and can be honest with you about whether you are a joy to be with or not! Prevention is better than cure and catching the downward spiral as early as possible is key to recovery.

But I just worry that . . .

> Whatever I do, I'm not going off with stress and depression – you are finished as a teacher when that happens.
>
> (Anonymous former colleague)

I wish I could say that my former colleague was wrong; unfortunately, although things are slowly changing, there is for some people a stigma about mental health. Having at one stage in my career worked in an institution where staff who were off sick with stress were prone to disappear without explanation, we certainly have a long way to go as teachers.

Whilst there are occasions when it is prudent to keep your head down and say nothing, if your health is being put at risk then this is no small thing that we are dealing with. To be blunt even if the worst happens and you are 'finished as a teacher', you will be alive and you will have your health. In most cases, it should not come to that. If it does, remember that you have a union and that your employer has both legal and moral duties towards you. Be prepared to fight your corner.

Stat attack

Suicide rates amongst teachers are 40% higher than the population as a whole (Illingworth 2010).

Onwards and upwards (or outwards)?

If, for whatever reason, you find yourself at rock bottom:

1   Get professional help if you need it. Your doctor, your union and counselling services such as the Teacher Support Network are there to help you. Refusing to use the help of others is stubbornness not strength; teachers can be more stubborn than most.

2   Take time off if you need to. You wouldn't feel guilty if you took a week off for flu or several weeks off recovering from a serious physical illness.

3   Get an outlet – find something that you enjoy away from teaching and give some time to that. It may be painting, playing the guitar or reading.

4   Surround yourself with positive people and avoid the negative.

And if onwards and upwards is not working, do you need to move out of where you are currently teaching? Remember school and college cultures vary greatly. Sometimes we can just be the wrong fit for the institution we are currently in.

1   If management are aggressive or bullying, keep a diary and record events; you may need it. Seek union advice discreetly. John Illingworth's report 'Reign of Terror' is a real eye opener on what is happening in some schools with regard to management style.

2   Make sure you remain employable by actively seeking CPD or developing sidelines such as examining. Try not to get trapped where you are.

? **Questions for reflection**

1 Have you had moments in your teaching career when you have been at rock bottom? How did you come through it? What support network do you have if difficult times come again?

2 Challenge: looking out for others. What random act of kindness could you do for a colleague in the next few days?

Bibliography

Illingworth, J (2010) *Reign of terror.* Available from http://www.teachermentalhealth.org.uk/Reign%20of%20Terror%20Final.pdf (Accessed 7th January 2016).

Part 2

Identity

Chapter 9

Teachers as persons – the philosophical bit

One of the more depressing phrases in the English language is the phrase 'human resources.' The phrase itself is a contradiction in terms. A resource is something that is used for a purpose, only has value when it is in use, and is disposed of the moment it ceases to be used. A human being is a person and should be subject to none of those things. Objects may behave in predictable ways and may be reliable to a point, but they have none of the spontaneity, creativity and autonomy of human beings. We are extraordinary, yet our systems in education, if we are not careful, have the potential to rob us, and our students, of our personhood. This chapter will help us to begin to think about our identity; by understanding what it means to be a person we will hopefully begin to value ourselves and others.

Philosophy corner – what is a person?

Philosophically the question of what is a person is not just an academic question. It has applications in topics such as abortion and euthanasia: is the foetus really a person? Is someone in a PVS state still a person? In debates on animal rights, concerns over the treatment of chimpanzees and dogs in experiments hinge on the fact that these creatures seem to have something more to them, something that resembles us, in a way that mice, fish and insects do not. Debates on equality are to some degree debates about personhood. The famous anti-slavery slogan 'Am I not a man and a brother?' is an appeal to be treated as full persons; something which the racist, the homophobe, the islamophobe rejects for certain groups.

Philosophers suggest lots of different criteria with regard to what makes someone a person: rationality, self-awareness, creativity, autonomy/free will, moral agency – the ability to make moral decisions, a being that can form relationships, a being that possesses rights and responsibilities. A precise definition of what makes a person is beyond the scope of this book, but the key point is this: persons are different from anything else in the world; they are extraordinary and we are persons!

> 'So act that you treat humanity, whether in your own person or in the person of any other, always at the same time as an end, never merely as a means.'
>
> (Kant 2002)

Persons – why does it matter?

Kant's rule that we should treat people as ends not as means can be stated in a more down to earth way – don't use people, respect them. This applies to ourselves and to others. Despite the best efforts of the powers that be to reduce education to a series of spreadsheets and graphs, this is ultimately a people centred business. People have rights and responsibilities; they deserve to be valued and treated with dignity. It is essential that we understand that both ourselves and others are persons and that we behave accordingly. In one interview I was once asked, 'What do you think of when you think of people?' The question stumped me at the time, but I think the answer I should have given is along the lines suggested above: people have value, are to be unconditionally respected, and have unlimited potential – for better or for worse.

Three persons to consider

1   **Consider our students**. They are persons. They may come to us with various backgrounds, SATs levels or GCSE scores that represent them as data, but they are each unique. They cannot be totally predicted; they do strange things – sometimes stupid, sometimes amazing. They surprise us and infuriate us in equal measure.

Whenever we say 'You should get this grade,' let's tread carefully and remember that this is a unique individual and not an object that we deal with. When we examine data, let's remember what it is that the data represents – the achievements and issues of persons. Dickens' character of Thomas Gradgrind who, in the novel *Hard Times*, insists on referring to 'girl number 20' (Hard Times, p. 14) is not intended as an example of good practice.

2   **Consider ourselves as teachers.** We are persons. We are not like an engine or a battery that can go on for days on end. There are times when we need a rest so that we have energy for the next day. Later on we will see that creativity demands a certain energy. We are not objects; we are capable of creative solutions to problems, we are able to sensitively pick up on moods and body language within the room and we tailor our approach accordingly. Just imagine the mess that would be made by a robot doing your job. Whilst it might not get tired or need sleep, the 'teacherbot' would be boring, predictable and would have no understanding of the human interactions that are at the heart of education and that ultimately cannot be measured.

3   **Consider your colleagues.** They are not objects. They need praise and encouragement. They need to feel that someone cares; that they are not just the 'body' that delivers a certain subject. Take an interest in them as people, particularly if you are a manager. If the only conversations we have with people are work related, we convey the message that only the work is valuable, not the person. Whether you are in leadership or not, a small act of kindness – such as taking in some cakes when everyone has had a hard week – speaks volumes.

Leadership byte

Clearly in terms of the role we play we can be seen as resources and fine ones at that! Yet to think of ourselves and others in that way is dehumanising and reduces people to mere objects. Who we are is far more important than what we do. Understanding the complexities and wonder of people is at the heart of our work. I would argue that if you don't value or enjoy people, you should consider whether you are suited for leadership or in fact for education at all.

Yes, but how? Practically speaking

- Relationships. Take opportunities to develop relationships. With your students, that might involve extra-curricular activities where they get to see you as a human being and you get to see another side of them. For staff, try where possible to get involved in staff social activities: take lunch in the staffroom, play football with colleagues after school one night, have breakfast together on Friday morning, go to the pub at the end of term. Join in; persons are built for relationships.

- Autonomy/freedom. Whenever possible, allow people choices. When disciplining students, link to choices they have made and offer a choice: 'I'd like you to choose to do this task, but if you choose . . .' etc. In class, can there be a choice of tasks? If you have some management responsibility, consider whether all staff need to do a certain thing in exactly the same way.

- Dignity. Above all, aim to be humane. Speak to the cleaners and canteen staff; make an effort to learn their names. Whilst I don't believe in karma as such, generosity and kindness do on the whole get repaid in the end.

You are not just a human resource. Keep in mind that you and others are persons. This one piece of information is your shield against much of the nonsense that is around in education.

> **?** **Questions for reflection**
>
> 1 How can you be more human with your students and the other staff? What can you get involved in?
> 2 How do you treat the support staff, such as cleaners, office staff and lunchtime supervisors? How can you make the working lives of these colleagues better?

Bibliography

Kant, I (2002) *Groundwork for the Metaphysics of Morals*. New Haven, Yale University Press.

Chapter 10

Teachers as persons – the practical bit

One of the perks of my role in recent years has been the opportunity to deliver sessions on staff training days. On one occasion when I felt that morale had been flagging for various reasons, I hijacked a session, as it were, to show staff a secret weapon. After 10 minutes explaining how we deliver exam technique to students, I introduced (after a big build up) the 'best resource in college'. It was in fact a mirror.

The point is really quite simple. We are the best resource that our students have. It's not the textbooks, YouTube, the computers or an iPad app. It's us. This chapter aims to build on the insight of the previous chapter that we are persons and considers what that might mean on a more personal level. Why and how can we begin to value ourselves as persons?

Losing our humanity?

Teaching can be a very lonely profession. You are alone in a classroom (with up to 30 students) for most of your working day and devoid of the company of other adults. There is no one there to look out for you, to tell you to go home early and take a night off. We are not machines that can carry on endlessly working at full speed, day in day out, year in year out. Often when we over extend ourselves, we start to fray around the edges; we lose it with those around us and we become slower, more irritable, and more random. It is not uncommon to see bizarre objects in strange places in the staff loos or staffroom. We are often in the midst of dashing from A to B whilst thinking about three or four other things that are urgent or pressing. Teachers often lose it in more ways than one!

Over the years I have seen colleagues with perfectionist tendencies suffer repeated ill health, talented colleagues simply leaving the profession and even a half consumed bottle of whiskey found whilst cleaning out a highly capable colleague's cupboards after he had left. As teachers we are incredibly giving people, but sometimes we need to give ourselves a break and be a little bit selfish for the sake of all those around us at home and at school.

Love yourself

Love your neighbour as you love yourself.

(The Bible)

If you are flying with small children, secure your own oxygen mask first before helping them.

(Various Airline Safety Announcements)

It is not wrong to value yourself and to consider your own needs. Even the Bible, with its challenge to love our neighbours, whoever they are, adds the words – as you love yourself. Valuing persons has to begin with our own self-image. We are intrinsically valuable; we are not just there to serve the needs of others. But if you do want a more practical reason to prioritise yourself – remember that you need to be looked after because of your value to your students.

If something is valuable you've got to look after it. If we were fortunate enough to own a Ferrari, I suspect we wouldn't use it for every trip from A to B; we would ensure it was well maintained, and it wouldn't do 50,000 miles plus a year! Yet we do this to ourselves. We push ourselves to the very limits. Remember we are the best thing that our students possess. If you don't look after yourself, then you do yourself, your family and ultimately your students no favours. As much as the other things – the technology and the textbooks – might enhance what we do, they wouldn't be able to operate without us there to facilitate. If everything else was stolen or destroyed, you would probably still be able to deliver the course with just a board pen. (I proved this during a recent power cut at college!) As teachers we are the Ferrari, or at least the engine of the Ferrari. If you were not there for any length of time, would the procession of supply teachers be able to do what you can do as well as you do it? It is not wrong to look after ourselves, and if we want to do our job well, it is wise.

Teacher 5 a Day

> If the collective minds in the profession can suggest that grading a 20 minute lesson is the work of fools, then surely we can do something about looking after ourselves a bit more.
>
> (Reah 2014, Para. 5)

One of the best campaigns to come from the Twitter education community in recent years is Martyn Reah's (@MartynReah) excellent Teacher 5 a Day idea to promote wellbeing. In his initial blog, cited above, he argues that it is the job of school leaders to look after their staff given that it is the staff that look after the students and their achievement. Using an amended version of Foresight and New Economic Foundation's 'Five Ways to Wellbeing' (2011), Martyn has encouraged a great number of teachers to reflect on their wellbeing by using the following headings:

- Connect. Develop relationships with significant others and meet new people online and in real life.
- Exercise. Take time to look after our physical health.
- Notice. Be in the moment and see what is around us, not mentally distracted by work 24/7.
- Learn. Keep growing and learning both professionally and personally.
- Volunteer. Give to others outside of work.

We will return to some of these themes later on, but these are good categories to consider when we reflect on whether we are looking after ourselves.

Yes, but how? Practically speaking – fix your dashboard

In a famous episode of *The Simpsons*, Homer, upon discovering that his wife Marge is pregnant with their third child, has to beg Mr Burns for his job back. Mr Burns proceeds to rub Homer's nose in it by putting up a plaque that reads, 'Don't forget, you're here forever.' When Maggie is born, Homer strategically covers various letters with pictures of his children so that the plaque now reads, 'Do it for her.' This will be his motivation for coming to work.

In their excellent A Level Mindset courses, Martin Griffin and Steve Oakes have a similar activity for students entitled 'fix your dashboard'. Whether it be your bedside table, your desk at work, or even the dashboard of your car, it is important that you have some reminders of your value, your value to others, and the need to look after yourself. It can be photos of your family, a few key words or a calendar with an anticipated date circled.

Don't see looking after yourself or your 'me time' as the least important item on your list. Looking after yourself enables the other things on the list to happen.

 Questions for reflection

1   Look at the five subheadings of the Teacher 5 a Day campaign. Which of these do you need to work on?

2   How can you fix your dashboard? What objects might help you keep things in perspective? Where will you put them?

Bibliography

Foresight and New Economic Foundation (2011) *Five ways to wellbeing.* Available from https://issuu.com/neweconomicsfoundation/docs/five_ways_to_well-being (Accessed 10th January 2016).

Oakes, S and Griffin, M (2016) *The A Level Mindset – 40 Activities for Transforming Student Commitment, Motivation and Productivity,* Camarthen: Crown House.

Reah, M (2014) *Teacher 5 a day.* Available from https://martynreah.wordpress.com/2014/12/06/teacher5aday (Accessed 10th January 2016).

Chapter 11

Understanding your purpose

> 'To forget one's purpose is the commonest form of stupidity.'
> (Attributed to Nietzsche)

One of the bestselling books of the last 15 years has been *The Purpose Driven Life* (2002). Its author, Rick Warren, founded Saddleback church in 1980 with a few members and has overseen its growth to over 20,000 members. At the inauguration of Barack Obama in 2009, Rick Warren was chosen to deliver the invocation. Key to the success of the church and the bestselling book, which is a study course on the idea of purpose, is the insight that organisations and individuals are more successful and happier when they have a clear sense of purpose or vision and everything they do moves towards that vision. Regardless of whether we have a faith perspective or not, there is something fundamental to our psychology here; we need a purpose and we need to be clear on our purpose. This chapter continues the theme of identity by reflecting on what our purpose is as teachers and how we can avoid what Nietzsche calls the commonest form of stupidity.

Teaching and purpose

In the business world, the more successful companies have clear ideas about where they are heading, and each employee is able to clearly explain how she or he fits into the whole. Likewise there is a great value in approaching the question of the purpose of our role as teachers. It is asking this question that enables us to rise above the day to day, with its relentless demands and the endless 'things to do' lists. Having a clear idea of the purpose of what we do each day can help us to sort out the treasure from the trash. To help us reflect on this, we can break the question down into three parts, each getting progressively closer to home: What is the purpose of education? What is my core purpose in my current job? What is my unique teacher 'shape'?

1 The global question: what is education for?

Great thinkers have long debated the purpose of education. Aristotle believed that education was about the development of the whole person. (SEAL and character education are not something new!) Its purpose was to prepare someone for living an 'excellent life'. For Plato there was an emphasis on the role of questioning and the idea of drawing out the answer already within through dialogue. (Perhaps he was the first progressive!) Knowledge and wisdom were valuable in their own right, yet there was also a sense that education enabled one to be prepared for a role within society; he was particularly concerned with preparing the philosophers to rule well.

In modern day America, the three aims of education given by Mortimer Adler in his 1998 work *The Paideia Proposal* were:

- the development of citizenship
- personal growth or self improvement
- occupational preparation.

Increasingly in Britain we have focused on the final one of these – the skills and employability agenda – and then become annoyed that schools have overlooked the first. Why haven't we taught them 'British values'? Nationally, internationally and possibly even in your institution there may be a confusion about exactly what education is for. Are we just training people for the jobs they will do? What about the two-thirds of their lives when they are not working? Should we also prepare them for that?

2 The local question: what is my job's core purpose?

Your contract probably has a whole list filed under job description of a range of tasks that you will be required to do. Some days it can feel like we are being asked to do them all on the same day. Yet the endless lists of things to do are not our purpose. Tasks are things that we may do in order to achieve a purpose. If we focus too much on tasks and targets, we are in danger of missing the wood for the trees. We need to answer the question 'why' before we can get down to the 'what'. Yet once we begin to grasp what our purpose is, then we can begin to get a sense of the relative importance of each task. It is then that we can begin to separate the important from the urgent and have the confidence to delegate or ignore those things which contribute nothing to the process. We will look at organising our time and tasks in more detail, using tools such as the Covey Quadrant in chapter 27.

3 The personal question: what is my teacher shape?

> Be your authentic teacher self. Make sure that you keep up to date with the latest research and thinking on education but then make this work for you.
>
> (Kidd 2014, p. 75)

We each have our own unique teacher style; in marketing terms, we have a USP. We all bring different things into the classroom and none of us would teach the same lesson or class in exactly the same way as someone else. This is why off the shelf lesson plans do not always work. What sort of teacher are you 'meant to be'? Borrowing and amending Rick Warren's (2002) SHAPE acronym, we can consider these five elements:

School – The context you are working in will affect purpose to some extent. If your school allows you to be your authentic self, you will be happier. If the school has different views on the purpose of education and how you should teach, it may be a struggle.

Heart – What are you passionate about? What things in education genuinely excite you? As an RE specialist, I love getting students to debate and think deeply about issues. Are there also passions from your life outside work that you could bring in?

Abilities – What are you particularly good at? This doesn't of course mean that you are excused from working on other things but our predominant style should be one where we play to our strengths. What we are good at is a clue to what we are meant to be.

Personality – You are an extrovert or an introvert; you may even have a Myers-Briggs type, complete with a list of its suggested strengths and weaknesses. Whatever it is, embrace it. If you are 'larger than life', go with it in the classroom. If not, develop the quiet and calm space in your room that reflects your personality.

Experiences – Our life before teaching and outside teaching shapes us. Often it is these experiences that help us to find our teacher purpose. Having a child with autism and being part of an organisation outside of college that has made excellent use of social media are just two of the things that have impacted my life as a teacher.

The question of purpose is the ultimate question. As individuals we need to answer that question: why do I teach? What am I doing this for? What is the unique teacher that only I can be? Our role in teaching gives us the fantastic privilege of helping to shape the next generation, of imparting something that will last long after we're gone. If life had turned out differently, we could have been selling products that we couldn't care less about for a faceless multinational. But we're not; we get the chance to help shape people's lives.

? Questions for reflection

1 Read and reflect on the purpose of education. What do you think? What does your school think? Are the two compatible?

2 If you had to sum up the purpose of your job in a sentence or two, what would it be? How do these relate to the purpose or mission of your institution?

3 What is your teacher SHAPE? What is it that only you can bring to the role?

Bibliography

Adler, MJ (1998) *The Paideia Proposal: An Educational Manifesto*, New York: Simon and Schuster.

Kidd, D (2014) *Teaching: Notes from the Frontline*, Camarthen: Independent Thinking Press.

Warren, R (2002) *The Purpose Driven Life*, Michigan: Zondervan.

Chapter 12

Vision and values

We'll go to epic lengths to fiddle controlled assessment. We'll enter whatever number we need to make the spreadsheet turn green regardless of whether a kid has done the work.

(Guardian 2014)

Assuming that we have a clear sense of why we are teachers and have some sense of our overall purpose, the next question is one of values. We know where we are going, but how exactly are we going to get there? What things do we count as being important as we aim towards our goal? Is it no holds barred – whatever it takes to achieve an aim – or are some things intrinsically valuable and non-negotiable in our value system? Having purpose alone is insufficient; all regimes have aims and goals. What is also needed is courage and a moral compass to navigate the educational winds of change. This chapter will focus on values; as persons we are, after all, moral beings. It is the values that we hold that inform how we approach our work and the methods that we employ in reaching goals.

The rise of pragmaticism

Without being idealistically naïve, stick to what you believe in rather than be a feather for each educational wind that blows – there are some things in education that are eternal verities.

(Tomsett 2015, p. 7)

Educational theories come and go out of fashion. Politically driven reforms come and go. Systems for determining success, league tables and performance measures change overnight. In many institutions, this has led to the rise of the manager without firm values who is happy to adopt whichever passing fad comes along. Schools and colleges have become difficult places to have values as whichever values you adopt can lead you to be flavour of the month one day and persona non grata the next. Yet John Tomsett is right, we have to be true to who we are. It is difficult to act against our values; it can harm our psychological wellbeing.

The danger of whatever it takes

To have goals without any values says that we will do whatever it takes, we don't care who we tread on, what rules we break, how many people we hurt along the way; we just want to get the job done. It is this pragmaticism brought on by league tables and Ofsted fear that drives many institutions. The second danger of pragmatism is that without clear vision or values we are prone to lurch from one strategy to the next without a clear sense of where we are heading or how we get there. Sometimes our experience is like that in George Orwell's *1984*: we hear in the staff meeting that we have 'always been at war with Eastasia' when it seems pretty clear that the opposite is true. Consider the following examples of pragmaticism in action:

The **C/D borderline** – We have identified a group of young people who are 'on the borderline'. These students have hit the jackpot in terms of interventions. There will be revision sessions galore, motivational speakers, small group sessions. What about the other students? Does every child matter?

Coursework – Neither Amir nor Belinda have any chance of achieving their qualification unless they have a little help with their coursework. When does that help cross the line? We all want the best for our students, but are we actually doing them any favours if we ensure they pass the course yet learn nothing? Recently an A level languages teacher spoke to me of his frustration in trying to teach A level French to students who had only got the GCSE thanks to an unexpected A/A* in their course-work. It is dishonest and merely passes the problem along.

Values are principles not rules

One problem you may spot with values is that they are slippery cus-tomers. They are actually very hard to measure. The dominant culture in education is one of rules and systems. These rules and systems are hard and fast. They enable measurement. They are inflexible when they are in force, yet they are jettisoned the moment that they do not seem to be reaching the goal. Hence these rules cannot be values; values are core principles, they are the things that are important to us regardless of whether they are convenient or not. One mantra has stuck with me from a training day early in my career: Not everything that can be mea-sured is valuable. Some things that are valued cannot be measured.

1 Personal values

Although our aims and objectives may change from year to year, our values are hopefully more constant. Organisations that succeed are very clear on both purpose and values; this is apparent both inside and outside education. In my present post when appointed as head of department I identified five values that were personal values but also encapsulated what was best about our department and that were non-negotiable in our pursuit of our goals. They were:

1   Passion – I want students to genuinely enjoy the subjects and engage with them. We aim to model this as staff. We aim to encour-age those students who are passionate.

2   Positive – It's amazing how different it is when you walk into the classroom believing that you can do it. We try to model positivity and encourage it in our students.

3   Excellence – If something is worth doing, it is worth doing well. Sometimes we can have so much to do that we approach each task half-heartedly; either do things well or leave them alone.

4   Responsibility – When students fail to show responsibility, we can compensate by working harder and doing things for them. It takes

courage (sometimes more than I possess) to stand back and expect them to do things themselves. Take responsibility in the staff room too. Are you worried about staff morale? Stop blaming the management; take the initiative and bring in some cakes.

5   Respect – It's obvious that genuine respect for colleagues and students is important. Equally there is respect for yourself and your family.

These values, although flexible in their application, inform our entire decision making. Identify the values that matter to you. They are key to understanding your identity.

2 Educational values

What do you believe about some of the great educational debates?

- Are you a traditionalist or a progressive? This is perhaps one of the liveliest debates in the educational community and perhaps the easiest one to start a fight with on Twitter! Broadly speaking, traditionalists think the role of teachers is to impart knowledge; they may favour direct instruction and textbooks and assess knowledge using tests. A progressive sees students as active participants in learning and plans child centred group activities that develop skills more than knowledge. Of course, the above is an over simplification, but it is important that you read, think and take a view. Personally I take the best of both!

- Where do you stand on educational technology? It may depend on where you teach. Is technology a massive distraction that makes it difficult for students to concentrate for any length of time or just a babysitting device that weaker teachers use to pacify difficult groups? Or could it be that technology is the most exciting educational development for generations? Is it the case that the opportunities for flipped learning and the widescale availability of so much free knowledge will change how we teach significantly and for the better? Again it is important that we take a view.

Remember if you don't think or research some of these areas for yourself, you may be prone to swallowing whatever you are told without thinking!

And finally

Whatever we have as our core values and beliefs, it is important that we live them. Both the staff and the students in our schools are watching, and they will learn and assume your values from what you do and don't do rather than from what you say.

 Questions for reflection

1 What are your values? What things are non-negotiable for you? How do they relate to your school's values?

2 Read about some key educational debates. What are your teacher values? Understanding issues and taking an evidenced view will shield you against the changing winds of policies.

Bibliography

Guardian (2014) *Secret teacher – Cheating schools targets results.* (18th January 2014). Available from http://www.theguardian.com/teacher-network/teacher-blog/2014/jan/18/secret-teacher-cheating-schools-targets-results (Accessed 16th January 2016). Courtesy of Guardian news and media Ltd.

Tomsett, J (2015) *This Much I Know about Love Over Fear,* Camarthen: Crown House.

Chapter 13

Identity theft – not just a teacher

> I hear colleagues saying: 'I'm just a primary teacher'. The ease with which some teachers, in a sense, put themselves down is quite telling.
>
> (Rogers 1992, p. 9)

Bill Rogers is right that it is sometimes the little words in our sentences that give the game away as to how we're thinking. How often we hear ourselves and others saying, 'I am just a teacher.' The word 'just' is interesting and in many ways more harmful than it first appears.

First, I am 'just a teacher' implies an inferiority complex. 'Just' in this sense means 'only'. Surely if we believe in our role as teachers, there is no 'only' about it. We have been educated to degree level, trained to manage a classroom and been appointed and trusted with improving the lives of young people – no pressure then! Let's not diminish our own significance by saying that we are 'just' teachers.

Second, and more seriously, 'I am just a teacher' seems to imply that this is all there is to me. I am nothing else other than my job. This chapter focuses more on this second issue as we continue to reflect on the idea of identity. To what extent can be ensure that our identity is not drowned out by the job that we do?

Identity theft or identity giveaway?

In one sense I am not a teacher. I have certificates that indicate otherwise and have wage slips, resources and other assorted stuff that suggest that this is how I have spent my time for almost 20 years.

What I mean to say is this – I am not *just* a teacher. It is not the whole story. I am a husband, a father, a son, an examiner, a writer, member of various groups. The label 'teacher' only describes part of me. It is not the sum total of my identity. I am a person who carries out the role of teacher and invests much of his life in ensuring that the role is carried out to the best of his ability, but, in terms of who I actually am, I am not *just* a teacher.

Don't get me wrong. We are rightly proud of the job that we do, but it is not our life; sometimes we carry on as though it is, as though there is nothing else to us, as though our whole identity is found in the classroom. Slowly but surely, our identity is stolen. Conversations with many colleagues suggest that this experience is far from unique. Many of us have suffered from identity theft and worry that the rest of our identity has become submerged into the word 'teacher'.

To be fair, 'stolen' is probably the wrong word. We voluntarily or at least subconsciously give it away. It's easy to do it, to forget that our work is not us. The job we do matters, and it's important we do it well. However, particularly in term time, we invest so much time into the job that we often end up becoming the job.

Identity theft – spotting the signs

We are all on a journey with this, and I have to be honest and admit that I'm not the finished article when it comes to this issue. Here are a few things I've noticed about times when I have begun to lose my identity:

1   **Criticism** – We become even more sensitive than usual to criticism! We forget that a criticism made in an observation about an aspect of our performance is just that and not a direct assault on us as a person. If someone criticises an aspect of your performance in the classroom (or, more accurately, a comment is made that you perceive to be critical) it is important to remember it is just that: a comment on how you have done an aspect of your job. You are not perfect nor should anyone expect you to be. One of our problems as teachers is that our identity and how we feel about ourselves is often wrapped up in how well we do our job, or how well we are

perceived to be doing our job. Remember, just because someone thinks you should have done something better does not necessarily mean that person is right. Even if they are right, that doesn't mean you aren't doing the rest of the job pretty well. Remember that criticism is hardly ever intended to be personal.

2   **Contentment** – When we are beginning to lose 'identity', we begin to lose contentment. It is important that we learn to be content in what we've done. Unfortunately for some, contentment has become synonymous with complacency. Yet most teachers are far from complacent. Teachers seem to have a default setting that drives them to be perfectionists. Aiming for excellence is one thing, but driving ourselves mad and wearing ourselves out ultimately achieves nothing for us; nor does it benefit those that we teach. It is important to remember that teaching is a marathon not a sprint; the best thing we can do for our students is to stay fit and well for the full academic year. Sometimes it takes courage to stop and say, 'This isn't perfect, but it's good enough. I need to stop now so that I am fresh for the next day.' If your lesson isn't perfect, that is often just as much a reflection of the constraints that you are working in as it is of your skills as a teacher.

3   **Cultivate** – When we are immersed too deeply in our teacher identity, the other aspects of our lives start to resemble plants that need watering! It is important to cultivate other aspects of your identity. Deliberately do other things that are not related to work. Plan an evening with the children, have someone round for a meal, take up a hobby and plan time to do this, learn new skills. Of course, as dedicated teachers, we will probably protest that we don't have time for such things, but let's think about that one. Are we really saying that our role as a teacher is so important that everything else has to be put on hold? And if so, until when? Our students connect with us as people and, if all we are relates to the job we do, then slowly but surely we will start to die inside. We will become less interesting and less effective. A well rounded person makes a better teacher.

Teaching is a highly skilled job. We are also more than teachers; we are not just the job we do. Be aware of times when you are a little more sensitive than usual to criticism and aim to balance the pursuit of excellence with the wisdom of contentment so that you can preserve your energy.

? Questions for reflection

1 Imagine that you are not a teacher. What will you do for a living? Imagine you are retired. How are you going to fill your days once the washing up is done and the bills have been paid? If you find this challenge difficult, could it be that you are too wrapped up in your identity as a teacher to enjoy the rest of life?

2 If someone asked you what your hobbies or interests are, what would you say? Would it take a while to answer? What might that reveal?

3 What aspects of your non-teacher identity do you need to develop or rekindle?

Bibliography

Rogers, W (1992) *Managing Teacher Stress*, London: Prentice Hall.

Chapter 14

Boundaries – knowing your limits

Where does your working life as a teacher end and the rest of your life begin? Suppose for the sake of argument it begins on Monday morning – let's say around 7:30 a.m. when you pull into the car park. (Perhaps it really began the previous day as you tried to plan a lesson, catch up with marking and show interest in what the kids were doing.) It is definitely a working day until you leave the building at 5 p.m. or whenever. Yet the day is not over; you may get out some work once the kids have gone to bed. The 2013 workload diary referred to in chapter 3 identifies that 23.8% of primary and 21.4% of secondary teachers' hours (14 and 12 hours a week respectively) occur out of hours: before 8 a.m., after 6 p.m., or at weekends. Even when we are not working, our minds are often mulling over the events of the day or anticipating the challenges of tomorrow. This chapter looks at one of the key challenges in our identity: securing a boundary between work and the rest of our lives.

How hard do we really work? The hours

As we are rarely switched off, even when not working, it is incredibly difficult to figure out where work ends and the rest of life begins; the workload diary suggests figures of 59 hours for primary and 56 for secondary. Whilst it may not be possible to get an accurate figure, let's suppose that this is broadly right. Even assuming that the teacher does no work at all during holidays, that would equate to between 2,180 and 2,300 hours each year (56×39 and 59×39, in case you ask!).

So how does that compare to other professions? Depending on who you believe, the average hours worked per year in the UK are between 1,650 (Stephenson 2012) and just under 2,000 (Daily Mail 2016). This figure has apparently come down from around 2,200 hours in 1950. So whilst the rest of the workforce have experienced a reduction in the hours spent working, it's probably fair to say that teachers' working hours have increased over the years; the 2010 equivalent of the workload diary cited 50 hours per week. Anecdotally this squares with my own experience and speaking to others. When I first entered the profession, some of the older colleagues I spoke to recalled a day circa 1960s/1970s when it was not unusual to see their older colleagues leaving the building 5 minutes after the pupils and carrying absolutely nothing.

The case for boundaries

The list of things to do will never be complete, and the UK requirement that teachers work 1,265 hours and 'whatever else is needed' is as hopeless as you can get. It is complicated all the more in the age of e-mail and remote access to school and college networks. Given that it is highly unlikely that anyone is ever going to come to us telling us to work fewer hours or to go home early, it falls upon us as professionals to have the confidence to set our own boundaries. However, determining where reasonable boundaries lie is harder than it first appears. Clearly sticking rigidly to 1,265 hours (which would be 32 hours each week in term time) is impossible. In my experience anyone who tries to argue for this probably doesn't have the best interests of their students at heart. Our students deserve our commitment, but so do our families and friends. Hence we recognise that we may need to work long hours, but how do we decide the limits?

Leadership byte

Although this is not embedded in many institutions, there are schools and colleges that have tried to put clear boundaries in place. At Quinton Kynaston, where @teachertoolkit Ross McGill is deputy head, a wellbeing bell sounds at 6:00 p.m. to encourage

---

any staff still in the building to consider going home. Recently headteacher Flora Barton (2015) blogged about putting staff well-being at the top of the agenda and the benefits this has had on results. One wellbeing measure is to ensure that staff go home before 4:15 p.m. on at least two nights.

50 is plenty!

The *Economist* (2014) blog 'Proof that You Should Get a Life' cites the research of John Pencavel at Stanford University. The research, although admittedly carried out in the manufacturing sector, shows that productivity and efficiency starts to decline once the 50 hour boundary is hit. Between 50 and 55 hours, workers are less efficient and productivity decreases; they are only marginally more productive than if they had worked 49 hours. His study showed that those who worked 56–70 hours added nothing as a result of their extra hours. Beyond 55 hours is a complete waste of time. Most of us intuitively know this, yet the culture of our schools dictates that we plough on; we have made a virtue of working every hour, and we reward those who seem to be best at it with promotion.

Establishing boundaries

Establishing our boundaries is much easier said than done, but here are some practical thoughts about how we might achieve it:

1   **Boundary of the day – time not task** – One way of fixing boundaries is to think in terms of the time taken rather than the task. Instead of saying 'I will work until I have X, Y and Z done,' how about 'I will be working from 8:00 a.m. until 6:00 p.m. today' (or 8:00 a.m. until 4:00 p.m. then 7:00 p.m. until 9:00 p.m.). Often as teachers we think in terms of tasks. We have a list of things to do, but the list is endless. A typical day involves crossing three things off, adding four more, and not getting any further on the remaining ten because we happen to be teaching most of the day. When we are task oriented, we tend not to notice the time slipping by

and we only stop work when we have completed a certain number of tasks. Having a time limit focuses us. If we measured our working day in terms of time, would we really get less done?

2   **Fix your boundaries** – One of the beauties of our job is that we do have some degree of autonomy; we don't do fixed shifts. If we were to work 50 hours each week, when would those hours be? What works best for you? Some people aim to do all their work at college, arriving early and perhaps leaving late. Some people work at home early mornings or evenings and aim to keep the weekends free. Personally I aim to start at around 6 a.m. most weekday mornings and to work one or two evenings at the most. Usually this keeps my weekends free, and the total adds up to around 50. There is more on how to organise your hours in chapter 33.

3   **Plan your time off** – Hopefully having a limit will give you time off to rest, enjoy your family and develop other aspects of your identity. It may sound counterintuitive, but for many of us, working less would actually make us better teachers. Choosing to limit the time spent working is not laziness but shows wisdom, confidence and maturity.

4   **Have a clocking off ritual** – As you leave work for the evening, try to do something that enables you to make the switch between work mode and off-mode. Bill Hybels' finishing points are described in chapter 21.

5   **Electronic boundaries** – Nowadays we have devices that make it difficult for boundaries to be maintained. The French government may well have passed a law preventing work emails after a certain time, but your students and possibly staff will send you work and raise queries at all sorts of hours of the day. Turn off the notifications on your devices and – I know they're addictive – avoid checking emails constantly. Also, if you are sending emails, think about the boundaries of others; save the email and send tomorrow or schedule a delivery time.

It is worth noting that a boundary is a theoretical division between two things. Until you actually step over it, it doesn't actually mean anything. Many of us physically leave work each day, but our minds are still there. Try to do something that helps you to switch off: a computer game, a favourite TV programme, a favourite CD on the way home, coffee with your partner. Do something that helps your mind to make the jump.

? **Questions for reflection**

1 Think about your last few weeks. If you have worked significantly over 50 hours, what did those extra hours add? How efficient were you?

2 As an experiment, plan your working hours for the next week and try to cut it to 50 hours. Then, after the week has passed, take note. What do you notice about your energy levels? Have you really gotten far less done?

Bibliography

Barton, F (2015) *Make 2016 the year you get the balance right.* Available from https://headsmart.wordpress.com/2015/12/28/make-2016-the-year-you-get-the-balance-right/ (Accessed 6th January 2016).

Daily Mail (2016) *Britons 'working more than 48 hours a week'* Mail Online. Available from http://www.dailymail.co.uk/news/article-98342/Britons-working-48-hours-week.html (Accessed 14th February 2016).

The Economist (2014) *Proof you should get a life.* Available from http://www.economist.com/blogs/freeexchange/2014/12/working-hours (Accessed 14th February 2016).

Stephenson, W (2012) *Who works the longest hours?* Available from http://www.bbc.co.uk/news/magazine-18144319 (Accessed 25th January 2016).

Chapter 15

The myth of work–life balance

> In summary, I think that I could and should have done better. Often, I didn't strike the right balance between work and home, and it is fair to say that our family life would have been richer if I had replicated the effort I put into work.
>
> (Grix 2016)

In the moving TES article quoted above, Principal Stephen Grix reflected on his own lack of work–life balance which was magnified by his wife's tragic death from cancer a year or so before he was due to retire. Indeed, as the old saying goes, none of us will, when we reach the end of our time on earth, wish that we had spent more time at work. However, that is not to dismiss the value of work and its role in making us the person that we are. This chapter looks at the Holy Grail that is work–life balance and considers how we might move closer to achieving it.

Work as part of life

Question: which of the following diagrams best reflects your understanding of the relationship between work and life?

1

The idea of a complete work–life separation is perhaps what we hope for when we think of work–life balance. Whilst that may been the experience of my father, who, once he had done his 8 hour shift down the mine, would come home, his work having no further impact upon him than requiring a brief snooze in the chair, this is probably wildly optimistic for teachers.

2

The second experience, which is common to many teachers, is what I call work–life encroachment. Work and its demands seem to tread all over the rest of life. Other life seems reduced in contrast. It is this experience that is causing many teachers to either leave teaching or to resent their work. Neither of these things is great for them or their students.

3

Replacing work–life balance in some circles is the idea of work–life merge. Here, particularly amongst millennials, work and life are seamlessly blended together via the laptop and smartphone; some work is done flexibly at home, business calls are answered whilst in the park with the children and e-mails dealt with between the main course and dessert in the local café. Whilst this may work for some office and business jobs, it is hard to see how this could work for teachers. The intensity of the job and the seemingly endless nature of it mean that, as argued in the previous chapter, some boundaries need to be drawn.

4

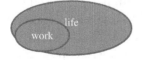

This fourth diagram perhaps best illustrates what is meant by work–life balance. Work is not something different to the rest of life. It is life, and it is where we are able to find some meaning and be useful to those around us; one of our key human needs

involves purpose and meaning. As attractive as a life of total pleasure sounds initially, we would get bored! Yet work is not the sum
total of our life, and it is important that we safeguard the division
between the two.

The value of work: useful work versus useless toil

In his famous essay, the Victorian writer William Morris outlines the
difference between useful work and useless toil. The three aspects that
make work useful are 'hope of rest, hope of product, hope of pleasure
in the work itself; and hope of these also in abundance and of good
quality' (Morris 1888, p. 2).

The nature of teaching as a profession means that our work is useful, assuming that we can get sufficient rest to recover our strength
and enjoy the process. We do see an end product, even if we are aware
that measuring it is a complex business; hopefully most days are var-
ied, and we can take pleasure in what we do. Part of a balanced life
is to enjoy and see the value of what we as teachers do. When we
overbalance and all we do is work, we can come to resent the job, yet
there are few professions that can claim anything like the impact that
we can have on the lives of others. Just a casual glance at the laptops
of the people around us on the train will show us the dullness of some
of the other jobs out there. Despite the best efforts of governments,
Ofsted and sometimes our own senior management teams, our work
is undeniably useful and is part of our lives.

Philosophy corner: Is teaching a vocation?

It is not unusual to come across earnest individuals who tell us
that teaching is not a job, it is a vocation. I am not convinced that
this is entirely helpful. The term 'vocation', meaning an occupation
that someone is drawn to in some way or especially suited to, has
a Christian origin and was primarily used to describe those going
into ordained ministry – they were called by God to their work.

Whether or not God has had any influence on our choice of
career, the parallels are unhelpful. A vocation IS your life, and
you sacrifice all manner of things, such as marriage or putting

down roots, in order to fulfil your calling. As much as our job is important, I am not convinced that 'vocation' is a helpful word; it has a tendency to be abused by those wishing us to work just that little bit harder.

The value of life: work in its place

Of course a balanced life has so much more going on than work. Perhaps, as for me, the quote at the start of the chapter resonates with you. We can be highly disciplined and organised at work, yet haphazard and laissez faire in the rest of our lives. Perhaps the exertions of endless target chasing and action planning leave us tired and resistant to attempts to structure what remains.

Whilst it is important to have times when we rest and recuperate, as will be argued in later chapters, it is important that we also use the time spent not teaching productively. Although I am not suggesting anything like a performance management review, it is worth spending some time reflecting on our aims for other areas of our lives. Ask yourself, for each area in the list below, two questions: What do you want to achieve? How will you do it?

- Health – Am I due any medical checks or appointments? How healthy am I and what am I going to do about it?
- Relationships – What will we do in the next couple of months to sustain the romance in our relationship? What will I do to develop certain friendships? How can I spend more time with my children? What family outings or treats will there be?
- Household and finance – What is the most urgent DIY project? Have we got the cheapest energy supplier? Where shall we go on holiday? (Plan ahead.) Since an unfortunate 3 months where we accidentally paid two electricity suppliers at once, my wife and I have a brief 'business' meeting each month in which we check in on these things!
- Hobbies and fun – What things will you do to bring joy to your soul? What things are you looking forward to?

Studies show that where goals are written down or shared with someone else we are more likely to stick to them. The process of writing or journaling may help us to reflect on where we are at in terms of our work and our life as a whole. It can also help to have someone to whom you are responsible and they to you. Ask each other the challenging questions about work–life balance.

Because the job we do is so important and useful, it isn't left to chance, and we have to plan and set targets. Yet we are also valuable, and we have duties to our nearest and dearest as well as to ourselves.

? Questions for reflection

1 Which of the diagrams on the relationship between work and life best sums up where you are at present? Is it where you want to be? If you find yourself at times resenting your job, ask yourself why that is.

2 Would you say that the balance between work and life is a healthy one?

3 How healthy is the rest of your life? Are there areas that require some energy and attention? Use the questions in the chapter as prompts.

Bibliography

Grix, S (2016) *My advice to teachers before its too late: Find a healthy work life balance.* TES (5th February 2016). Available from https://www.tes.com/news/further-education/breaking-views/my-advice-teachers-its-too-late-find-a-healthy-work-life (Accessed 9th February 2016).

Morris, W (1888) *Useful Work v Useless Toil,* London: Penguin Books.

Chapter 16

Professionalism, perfectionism and presenteeism

> 'I don't know what you mean by "glory"', Alice said. Humpty Dumpty smiled contemptuously. 'Of course you don't – till I tell you. I meant "there's a nice knock-down argument for you!"'
>
> 'But "glory" doesn't mean "a nice knock-down argument"', Alice objected.
>
> 'When I use a word', Humpty Dumpty said, in rather a scornful tone, 'it means just what I choose it to mean – neither more nor less'.
>
> (Carroll 1871, p. 75)

It is easy to have some sympathy with the frustrations experienced by Alice. I have similar feelings over the much abused word 'professional,' a word that often means whatever the person using it wants it to mean. When we attempt to define our identity by setting clear boundaries that enable us to have a genuine work–life balance, it is not unusual for someone to suggest that something we have or haven't done is unprofessional. This chapter looks at what the word 'professional' may mean when applied to teachers and some of the things that it shouldn't mean.

It is unprofessional to . . .

Prior to writing this chapter, I thought it would be an interesting exercise to survey connections on social media regarding what understandings of the words 'professional' and 'unprofessional' were in their various settings. The more interesting findings are found in Table 16.1.

Table 16.1 What Does Professional Mean?

It is unprofessional to . . .	It is a professional expectation that teachers. . .
• Have tattoos or piercings • Join in playground games • Wear a hat on INSET days • Wear a top that does not cover the elbows • Wear headphones whilst in the departmental office • Leave a class whilst having a panic attack • Cry in the staffroom	• Remain on site for at least 30 minutes after children have gone home • Give up 2–3 days each holiday for unpaid revision/ masterclasses for students

Whilst, depending on context and circumstance, there may be merit in some of the items, what becomes evident after a while is that to some extent the definition of 'professional' is subjective. It is often about preferences and, at the risk of making an ageist comment, is more about what teachers did 'back in my day'!

Professional – the four P's that it isn't!

There are a number of misunderstandings of professionalism. Here are four of the most common:

1 Preference: As we have seen above, too often professionalism can simply be a matter of preference. It is as if the person demanding that you be more professional is merely saying, 'Why can't you be more like me?' However, to call things that we disapprove of unprofessional, and to praise things that we ourselves do, fails to recognise the differences among people. The passive-aggressive email that says X is unprofessional often says more about the sender that the one at whom it is aimed.

2 Phariseeism: Just as the Pharisees of Jesus' day were accused of 'straining out gnats but swallowing camels,' so too a legalistic focus on keeping lots of different rules usually ends up missing the whole

point. Professionalism cannot be narrowed to a set of rules. Enforcing such rules, with about as much humanity as the average self-service checkout, risks engagement at the expense of compliance.

3   Presenteeism: One of the great diseases of many workplaces, not just in education, is presenteeism. Although mainly referring to attending work when ill, there is a broader definition which extends to putting in the hours and being seen to be present. This may be due to job insecurity but, more often than not, it is due to guilt and not wanting to be the one that 'lets the side down'.

4   Perfectionism: Perhaps underpinning all of the above, at least psychologically, is the notion of perfectionism. We as teachers are particularly prone to this. Yet the idea of professionalism has more to do with excellence rather than perfection. There is a difference.

Leadership byte: trust

Many of the above misunderstandings and misinterpretations of professionalism are driven by fear and the need to control. Leading people is scary and frustrating, yet trust is key. If you do not trust people and they realise that, you may get compliance on your rules, but you won't get engagement. Issue an edict that staff stay on site until 30 minutes after the students, and they will leave 31 minutes after the students and will resent your pettiness. Give trust and freedom; only take it back and 'have that conversation' if it is abused.

Professional – the three A's that it is

Professional: Having the qualities that you connect with trained and skilled people, such as effectiveness, skill, organisation and seriousness of manner (Cambridge Dictionaries Online, 2016). There are three attributes of a professional:

1   Autonomy – Professionals, unlike their blue collar clocking in and clocking off counterparts, have some degree of control over their working hours. Just as inevitably this means that they will

work late without the expectation of overtime, it should equally cut the other way. Professionals may, assuming they have no classes or other essential duties, choose to leave the building. Professionals are also trained to high levels in their fields, so they ought also to have some autonomy over their methods. If you have to be micromanaged and directed every few minutes, you are not really a professional.

2   Authoritative – Professionals have attained a level of expertise. They have, through their training and through keeping up with developments in their field, acquired the status of being an authority. This is why genuine CPD (as opposed to the prolonged PowerPoint briefing day) and a willingness to keep growing and learning is so vital to the profession of teaching. This is why disagreements between professionals should be resolved by humble reasoning and argument rather than appeals to authority. Professionals gladly change their methods when they are persuaded to do so by a fellow expert's logic; they resent being directed for seemingly no good reason.

3   Attitude – Professionalism is to some extent about actions, but it is far more about attitudes. A professional cares about the task in which he or she is engaged; it is more than merely a way to pay the bills. To be a professional is to some extent to be committed to going the extra mile; on occasions wisdom dictates pulling back in order to avoid burnout, but the commitment to doing the best job possible remains.

If we were to add a fourth point, more as a conclusion than as a separate idea, it would be this: be authentic. As professionals, we are not called to be perfect but to be as excellent as we can possibly be within the confines of our situation. Celebrate your successes, think seriously about your practice, and, as humbly as you can, keep trying to get a bit better.

Above all, focus on principles and attitude rather than rules. Aim to become an authority in your area. Take control and use what autonomy you are given for good ends. If you don't abuse your freedom, you may get more.

Bibliography

Cambridge Dictionaries Online (2016) Definition of professional. Available from http://dictionary.cambridge.org/dictionary/english/professional (Accessed 31st May 2016).

Carroll, L (1871) *Alice Through the Looking Glass*, London: Collins Classics.

Chapter 17

Confidence

8.30 a.m. on a Monday morning. Today I'm not feeling it. I look at my timetable and I just don't feel I can do this. I am not a very good teacher. I start to think about all the things that I don't do well. The day ahead looks like a mountain that needs to be climbed, a mountain in a vast Himalayan range called the academic year. I wrestle with these feelings throughout most of the day. Emotion vs evidence, and emotion threatens to win. The lessons go well, but the feeling is stubborn and isn't responding. The students seem to have enjoyed the lessons, but how can I be really sure they've learned anything? The mind runs wild. For the first time in 12 years I have had poor exam results this year. Although in the process of a formal appeal, it is a knock to confidence. Then I worry about my next observation, which is probably weeks away. What if it goes badly? What if I end up under capability procedure? What else could I do if teaching – my career for over 15 years – doesn't work out? I just can't do this . . .

Recently I stumbled upon a football phone in and heard the following story. Back in the days when Martin O'Neill was manager of Leicester City, after one heavy defeat in which the team – and, in particular, winger Steve Guppy – had played poorly. O'Neill told his team how poor they had been. Then, to the astonishment of everyone, he picked out Guppy and told him how well he had done in the game! The next game, Guppy was the star man and his form continued for much of the season. We can learn an awful lot from O'Neill's man management and about the value of that mystical property: 'confidence'. Confidence is such an important factor in any area. To believe that we can do something well and to know that others believe it of us is massive. This chapter concludes the theme of identity by looking at the shifting sands that are confidence; just what is it that we believe about ourselves and our abilities?

Voices – inside and outside our heads!

As a man thinketh in his heart, so is he.

(The Bible)

The man who says he can and the man who says he cannot are both correct.

(Confucius)

In our profession there is never a shortage of people queuing up to point out the things that we could do better. The media, inspectors, observers and managers will no doubt all have a view on what can be improved. Clearly they are often right to a point; none of us are perfect and we can always improve. Advocating confidence is not the same as defending blind arrogance; as Dylan Wiliam argues, 'Every teacher needs to improve, not because they are not good enough, but because they can be even better' (Wiliam 2012 cited in Tomsett 2013). Unfortunately the target driven culture that permeates the public sector forces us to dwell on those things that are not going well. We need to remind ourselves or have others remind us of all the good things we do each day.

In addition to the external voices, our own inner monologue is often not as helpful as it could be. In teaching four or five times each day, we set out, walk into a room and seek to impose our will upon a group of young people who may be anywhere on the scale between highly motivated to determined to make our lives a misery. In many schools, if students are generally compliant, we'll take that. To have the voice of self-doubt muttering away in your mind as you walk in doesn't help.

The effects of confidence and lack of confidence

The main effect of confidence or a lack of it shows itself most clearly in our thoughts about the future. When we lack confidence, the 'what ifs' that we mull over become more negative. Lacking confidence leads us to play it safe and focus on preventing things going wrong. A confident teacher experiments and takes risks, looking to actively make things go right. When we're confident, we walk with a spring in our step and we attempt greater things; sometimes they come off because we actually believe that they are possible.

Like many schools and colleges, we have recently moved away from high stakes graded lesson observations. All they told us were that scared, possibly under confident, colleagues could teach solid, safe and dull good lessons! The best teachers confidently take risks and we want to create space for that to happen even if that means that it won't always work.

Leadership byte

If you are a leader or manager, there is a lesson here. I'm not suggesting we praise poor performance in the way that Martin O'Neill did or that we let everything go, but when we do critique the work of others, we must always be mindful of confidence. Most of us will hand on heart know when we've put in a poor performance. There is a value in letting some of the little things go and being generous in our praise. You may just find that the increased confidence generated produces far more improvement than a telling off ever could!

Confidence and emotions

Over the course of any given day or week, our confidence goes up and down; it is emotionally driven and, like all emotions, it is involuntary and not always logical. Unfortunately we are prone to assume that the feelings are facts and select our facts according to our mood. We can be blind to our weaknesses because we are in a particularly buoyant mood; so too the arrival of the black mood can blind us to all our strengths. So how do we ensure that we handle these dips in confidence?

1   Challenge your emotions. Notice how you are feeling, by all means, but think about and, if necessary, challenge your emotions. Remind them of the evidence. Keep thank you cards, positive observation feedback and other reminders of what you can do. Make sure they are in a prominent place on your desk or in the office.

2   Surround yourself with supporters. Teaching can be a solitary job. You are a lone worker for most of your day. Make sure you spend time with colleagues who can build you up. It is easier to see the strengths of others than our own. What would these friends and colleagues say if only they knew how you felt? Find someone that you can share such things with.

3   Try to keep your equilibrium. It is harder to be rational and see things clearly when tired and stressed. As we will see in our next section, our energy level and our physical state can affect our thoughts and feelings considerably. The mind needs to be rebooted to its right state. An evening off, a half hour with a good book or some good music may be all it takes.

Even if you don't believe that teaching is a performance art, it is certainly true that it is one where you are on show all day and many pairs of eyes are trained on you. That's why confidence matters. If I could bottle one thing and give it as a gift to the nation's teachers, I would give them confidence.

? Questions for reflection

1   What negative thoughts do you find yourself thinking? Are there any obvious causes?

2   What evidence do you have of the good job that you often do? Are those things accessible or visible to you?

3   Given that acting confident can be the first step to real confidence, what can you do in terms of posture or actions that will enable your brain to think confidently?

Bibliography

Tomsett, J (2013) *This much I know about why all of us must improve our teaching.* Available from https://johntomsett.com/2013/01/05/this-much-i-know-aboutwhy-all-of-us-must-improve-our-teaching-no-matter-how-good-our-school/ (Accessed 31st May 2016).

Wiliam, D (2012) *How do we prepare our students for a world we cannot possibly imagine?* SSAT Annual Conference keynote, Liverpool, December. Available from www.dylanwiliam.org/Dylan_Wiliams_website/Presentations.html (Accessed 6th April 2016).

Part 3

Energy

Chapter 18

Energy – the magic ingredient

Case study: Geena's interview

The deputy headship of the local college seemed to be Geena's dream job. Once the essential tasks of her current position had been completed at around 4 p.m. that Thursday, she began to read through the college documentation, anticipate likely interview questions, and even more importantly, prepare the General Studies lesson she would be teaching. By 2 a.m. on Friday morning, everything was meticulously planned and she was ready. Just over 5 hours later she was on route to the interview. Needless to say the day was a disaster. The lesson went okay, but she spent much of the day seeming distant and disinterested. She didn't get the job.

We have all had days similar to Geena's. On one occasion in the days of graded observations, I was given the dreaded 'grade 3'. Once I'd calmed down, I had to agree. On that occasion I had prepared fully and had good resources, but I had also been away working all weekend for the exam board. Thus when things didn't go according to plan early on in the lesson, I was too tired to respond. I hadn't yet realised the significance of energy. The second main theme of this book is energy. These chapters look at how we can preserve our energy so that this magic ingredient in our teaching is not lost.

What is energy?

Energy is a magic ingredient: one that, in culinary terms, seems insignificant on the recipe yet, when it comes to the tasting, its absence is noticed. In teaching terms, there are days when you have a plan, have the resources and yet something is missing. Quite often that something is energy. Contrast that to other occasions, often without an observer present, where the lesson has been loosely planned but, crucially, energy was present. On those occasions where I have been 'inspiring', there has been energy in the teaching.

Our English word 'energy' comes from a Greek word 'energeia' which literally means 'operating' or, better, 'working in' something. It gives the idea that there is something that, when present, makes things work. The common definition from physics, 'the ability of a system to perform work', seems to also convey this sense.

In psychological terms it can be difficult to talk about energy without appearing a little mystical or vague. Yet both Freud and Jung wrote about 'libido' and intended this idea of energy or appetite to be wider than its current sexual connation.

Teaching as the 'energy hoover'

We have all heard of or met 'mood hoovers,' those people who drain us and suck the joy out of any room they enter. In a sense teaching has the potential to be an 'energy hoover'. We give energy to the process and we lose energy in the process. Sometimes we gain energy as our class contributes and gives back, but sometimes we just give – there are those lessons where we feel we are pushing water uphill. Consider the following factors:

1   The physical demands – Sometimes, particularly at the end of a full day's teaching, we can be physically drained. Having given everything to the process, we sit in the staffroom quite literally summoning up the energy to go home. Physically you can be on your feet all day moving at speed from one interaction to another with little rest. The physical demands of the job are considerably more than is realised from the outside. For those of us in teaching, the main

reaction, apart from despair, to the idea that teachers will retire at 68 has been bemused laughter.

2   The mental demands – Teaching is also mentally demanding. In *The Lazy Teacher's Handbook* (2010), Jim Smith points to research that suggests a classroom teacher may make 1,500 educational decisions each day: who to ask the question to, how to phrase it, where to stand in the room, how to explain a concept that has been misunderstood. Added to this is the difficulty that our day is not done when the day is done. We will probably have to take work home with us. It is no wonder that once you're home and being asked what you want for tea, it becomes an effort to respond. Psychologists refer to this as 'decision fatigue'.

3   The emotional demands – Teaching is an emotional job. You spend the day managing emotions, including your own. Emotional interactions can both give and take energy. A group that is quiet and sulky can require as much energy as one that is boisterous and challenging. We will look at the idea of managing emotions a little more in the next chapter.

Of course these are not three completely separate demands; they are linked and affect each other. In some ways teaching has a lot in common with performance, and performing is draining. You come off stage exhausted – possibly elated, but exhausted none the less.

The aspect of performance shows why energy matters in the classroom; you are not yourself in a classroom, you are a heightened version of yourself. You play a role where you respond to the other characters in the drama. You have prepared lines which you deliver with energy, but there are also the ad-lib responses where the success or failure of an interaction can hang by a thread.

'Manage your energy not your time'

The mantra 'manage your energy not your time', which seems to have its origins in the *HBR* article by Schwartz and McCarthy (2007), was something I first came across a couple of years ago. As someone who has reasonably good time management skills, I rejected this advice as misguided. Yet I was wrong; they are both important. Thinking in particular about the physical aspect of energy, there are four things that we can do to protect and enhance our energy levels:

1   Sleep – When we're busy, this is one of the first things to be squeezed. By working late or starting early, it is not unusual for teachers to have whole weeks of 6 hours' sleep a night. For me, the *Guardian* education article (Willis 2014) on teacher sleep was a wakeup call (if you pardon the pun!). Lack of sleep may significantly slow the mind down. I now try to ensure at least 7.5 hours sleep per night. Although my evidence is purely anecdotal, I reckon I teach much better when I've slept. So be brave; ignore those colleagues who seem to delight in boasting how late they were marking, and try an early night.

2   Water – Many teachers love coffee. We can be over reliant on it and wonder why we're sluggish in the afternoon. As teachers we can be particularly prone to dehydrating. We cannot just pop out of the office for a drink. Often break times can disappear into a choice between visiting the toilet or the water fountain by the time you have emptied your classroom. One way that I have tried to solve this is by adopting the early morning ritual of filling three bottles as soon as I get in. My aim is to drink all of them by the end of the day. When I manage this, I feel better.

3   Admin – We can't control our timetables, but we can decide when we do other tasks. Aim where possible to plan or mark when energy is relatively high (easier said than done). I tend to reserve data entry tasks or desk tidying for those moments past 5 p.m. when the mind isn't at its sharpest.

4   Fill your well – As well as trying to avoid the drain of energy, it is important to find time for things that increase energy. This could be exercise, time with the family, reading or socialising. A night off can do wonders for your ability to move through a 'things to do' list the next day. Try to clear at least one midweek evening completely each week and at least one day at the weekend. You will feel the benefit the next day.

? **Questions for reflection**

1 Have you had occasions where you have planned, yet in terms of your energy you are under prepared?
2 On average how much sleep do you get per night? Is it enough?
3 Which of your tasks are high energy tasks that require mental alertness and which can be done when you are half awake? When should each be done?

Bibliography

Schwartz, T and McCarthy, C (2007) Manage Your Energy Not Your Time. *Harvard Business Review*. Available from https://hbr.org/2007/10/manage-your-energy-not-your-time/ar/1 (Accessed 6th February 2016).

Smith, J (2010) *The Lazy Teacher's Handbook*, Camarthen: Crown House.

Willis, J (2014) *Teacher's guide to sleep – and why it matters* The Guardian website. Available from http://www.theguardian.com/teacher-network/teacher-blog/2014/nov/11/good-night-teacher-guide-sleep (Accessed 14th February 2016).

Chapter 19

Energy – emotional intelligence and burnout

As Bill Rogers notes in *Managing Teacher Stress*, the origins of the idea of 'burnout' come from a *Time* magazine article in 1981. 'It is characterised by high expectations, impatience, growing frustration, a fatigue that affects body and soul . . . a spiritual numbness and detachment' (Rogers 1992, p. 8). It is the cumulative effect of giving so much over a long period.

This theme is picked up by Laura McInerney, who writes about a growing group of experienced teachers who are leaving full time permanent teaching. They are 'tired of the responsibility that being a full-time employee in schools involves – particularly if they are trying to combine it with being a carer. For them, teaching has become too much. The learning walks, the parents evenings, the endless data entry. Fifty hour working weeks . . . work for some people. But no longer for them' (McInerney 2015).

Teacher burnout is unfortunately a real thing. Agi Enyedi's (2015) excellent article on the phenomena of teacher burnout notes that burnout affects the helping professions – those that spend energy meeting the complex demands of others. Burnout also creates prime candidates for chronic stress: whilst we are built to be resilient to short bursts of high stress, the longer periods of intensive high pressure work do not suit us as well! This chapter looks at how we can prevent or combat this by being more emotionally intelligent and paying attention to our energy in the long term.

Getting in touch with yourself: what is emotional intelligence?

Daniel Goleman's book *Emotional Intelligence* (1995) has, in addition to being a bestseller, formed part of reading lists for business leaders and managers for the last couple of decades. Unfortunately it does not seem to have found its way to all educational leaders, if some of the anecdotes found whilst researching this book are true.

Goleman's key idea is that intelligence and technical skill are not necessarily the main things that predict success; to be truly successful, a person needs to have emotional intelligence. Table 19.1 summarises what Goleman, in the January 2004 edition of *Harvard Business Review*, identifies as the five key components of emotional intelligence in the workplace.

Table 19.1 Features of Emotional Intelligence

Component	Description
Self-awareness	The ability to recognise and understand your moods, emotions and drives; the ability to understand their effect on others.
Self-regulation	The ability to control or redirect negative or disruptive impulses or moods; being able to suspend judgements and think before acting.
Motivation	A passion to work that is not connected to money or status; pursuing goals with energy and persistence.
Empathy	The ability to understand the emotional make up of other people; being skilful in treating others according to their emotional reactions.
Social skill	Skilled in managing relationships and building networks; able to find common ground and build rapport with others.

(Adapted from Goleman 2004)

These skills and the extent to which we possess them are part of our personality and nature, but they can be trained. We can become more emotionally intelligent.

Personally speaking: 15 years and two stories

Early on in my career, returning after 2 days off with a virus, I was confronted by the head of year and told that my register was a mess; could I please tidy it? The result was that I entered my first lesson fuming and managed to get into a confrontation with a difficult student with whom I had previously built a good relationship. I ended up having to apologise and spent the next couple of months rebuilding the relationship.

Fifteen years on – just last month, in fact – I found myself in a classroom similarly frustrated as a result of a couple of errant students from a previous lesson. I noticed a mobile phone being used at the back of the room and asked the student to stop texting in class. 'I'm not texting, I'm on Facebook,' came the reply, with a smile. This time I recognised my emotional state and, after calmly explaining that the action was unacceptable and demanding that the offending object be put away, I walked away. It may have taken 15 years, but I'm learning.

Emotional intelligence and energy

Once we understand a little more about emotional intelligence and its impact on energy, a few ideas become clear:

1   Know yourself – The key message that the idea of emotional intelligence brings to the table is the need for us to be aware of and regulate our emotional states. Emotional reactions can drain us of energy and over time can wear us down. To use an analogy, If we don't notice how low our fuel gauge is, we are more likely to run out of fuel. Often that seems to be what burnout and long term stress leave is: a running out of the fuel of energy.

2   Build in a pause – Goleman (1995) and Peters (2011) remind us that our emotional thinking is quicker but sloppier than our rational brain. Pausing before reacting in class and in meetings and, where possible, delaying a decision when we are feeling emotional are vital skills and cannot be overestimated. You are then in a better position to establish whether you are right to feel angry, hurt or disappointed and can respond intelligently. This is one way of preventing the drain of emotional energy.

3   The moment will pass – Teaching is to some extent a performance art, and finishing a teaching day often feels like coming off stage. Based on my own limited experience of performance and reading about other performers, coming off stage is a bizarre combination of being both 'buzzing' and 'shattered'. It is not unusual, following such a giving of energy, to have a low period following it. Indeed the nineteenth century preacher Charles Spurgeon spoke of his 'blue Mondays' following the exhilaration of speaking to thousands several times each Sunday. Accept the emotion, but also accept that it is likely to pass.

4   Routines – Look for shortcuts in your routines. For example, can you cut down on duplication? What about voice recorded feedback on work? More on this in Part 4 of this book.

Leadership byte

As a leader you have the ability to create and change the climate of your school or college. This is particularly so when it comes to the issue of communication. If you have to deliver bad news, the morning briefing probably isn't the place. The people you have just demoralised will have to go out and teach that day. If the issue only involves two or three staff, does everyone need the email?

Gaining energy

Avoiding burnout isn't just a matter of preserving energy; we can gain energy as well. Look for things that will allow you to restore your energy levels

1 Rest. This is the obvious one and will be covered in the next few chapters. Remember also your physical energy as mentioned in chapter 18 – sleep, water and the gym!

2 Reading or drinks? It is worth reflecting on whether you are an introvert or an extrovert as this may affect what energises you. Quizzes such as the Myers-Briggs temperament analysis can give you an insight if you are not sure. As an introvert, time spent alone reading, listening to music and reflecting gives me energy. Social interactions can be quite tiring. For more extrovert colleagues, a weekend spent socialising with others can restore energy levels. Know yourself.

3 Have an outlet. Having an interest outside of work is essential – it may even be related to education, such as writing/blogging. It is so easy for teaching to be all consuming, yet if we don't want to be 'consumed', we ought to have something else going on. Personally speaking this has been one of the features of times in my career where I have become stressed or tired: the decline of hobbies and interests.

4 And if you must work: For those times when you just have to put in the hours, notice that some aspects of the job are more fun than others; they are closer to your passions and motives. (Remember your teacher SHAPE.) When you have to take work home or lose half your weekend, try to lose it on the parts of the job you enjoy, so it won't sap your energy quite as much. For most of us, that means do some creative planning and leave the marking until Monday.

? Questions for reflection

1 Look at the table of emotional intelligences. Which do you do well and which do you need to work on?

2 How can you build in a pause before reacting? How might this work in the classroom and with decisions outside class?

3 Are you an introvert or an extrovert? What types of things restore your energy levels?

Bibliography

Enyedi, A (2015) *How can teachers avoid burnout?* Available from https://www.
britishcouncil.org/voices-magazine/how-can-teachers-avoid-burnout (Accessed
6th April 2016).

Goleman, D (1995) *Emotional Intelligence – Why It Can Matter More Than IQ,* New
York: Bloomsbury.

Goleman, D (2004) What Makes a Leader. *Harvard Business Review.* 82(1): 82–91.

McInerney, L (2015) *Why tired teachers might hold the clue to the teacher shortage.* Schools Week 26th November. Available from http://schoolsweek.
co.uk/why-tired-teachers-might-hold-the-clue-to-the-teacher-shortage/?utm_
content=buffer28131&utm_medium=social&utm_source=twitter.com&utm_
campaign=buffer (Accessed 29th December 2015).

Peters, S (2011) *The Chimp Paradox,* London: Vermilion.

Rogers, W (1992) *Managing Teacher Stress,* London: Prentice Hall.

Chapter 20

Be positive

> You see things; and you say, 'Why?' But I dream things that never were; and I say, 'Why not?'
>
> (Shaw, 1949, p. 7)

The morning papers are leading with yet another thing that teachers do badly. The staff briefing informs you of the thing your school isn't doing well enough according to Ofsted. A senior manager stops you in the corridor and tells you that Abi's parents have rung and asked why you haven't marked her homework. All this before you get to the classroom. In your room are students who tell you they can't do some of the work. At the end of the day you become aware of some of the things you haven't done or haven't done as well as you could. As teachers we are exposed to a considerable deal of negativity most days, and it takes a great deal of energy to remain positive; we are swimming against the tide. Yet, in the long term, optimism beats pessimism. This chapter looks at the importance of being positive and how we can remain positive in spite of it all.

The effect of negativity

> Teachers suffering from burnout view personal accomplishment negatively: they don't set goals and have low self confidence.
>
> (Enyedi 2015)

The positive thinking bandwagon has of course been much abused, and there are many consultants who have made a great deal of money selling snake oil type optimism which in effect denies reality. However, research by Fredrickson and colleagues (2008) suggests there is a significant degree of truth in the claim that positive thinking helps us. In order to understand this, it is necessary to look at how negative thinking arises. Negative thinking is a response to threat and dangers. Our focus narrows on combating the danger, and we don't notice anything else. Our world literally narrows. The analogy given by writer James Clear is to imagine you are being chased by a tiger. You are unable to think or notice anything else (Clear 2013). Whilst this adaptation of our brain is useful for crisis situations, it is not always helpful in the everyday.

For us as teachers most situations that we face are not life or death crises but are complex situations that are open to a variety of interpretations. The glass may be half empty or half full, but the evidence suggests that our brain genuinely shows us the world differently when we are negative. Our focus narrows and we miss bits. We are creating a reality rather than viewing it. Remember that the chimp that we referred to earlier is prone to catastrophic thinking and that the brain, as Goleman says, is prone to quick but sloppy emotional thinking.

This is why the idea of 'noticing' is so important and is one of Martyn Reah's Teacher 5 a Day. It is ironic that our target setting culture actually requires us to narrow our focus on specific things that are not going well. In doing so, how many good things do we miss?

Why we need to be positive

Research seems to show that positive thoughts can genuinely improve your state of mind and the quality of your life. The other side of the research carried out by Fredrickson and colleagues is that positive emotions can actually broaden people's attention and thinking (Fredrickson et al. 2008, p. 2). They broaden the sense of the possibilities; they literally open your mind. This in turn seems to facilitate more personal growth in terms of building personal skills. With an open mind we can, in the words of George Bernard Shaw, focus on the possibilities before us rather than narrowly focusing on the problem in hand.

The importance of hope

Teaching can be wearing at the best of times, but it is absolutely miserable if you have lost hope. Hope is future focused. It takes the 'what if' question and, instead of presenting us with a worst case scenario, it presents a pleasant possibility. What actually could happen if things went really well? Too often we can be guilty of worrying about what could go wrong so much that we don't step out and do things that could make things go right:

1   We need hope for ourselves. We need to be able to see what we can do. Just because something hasn't worked once does not mean it will never work. The past need not always resemble the future. If we lose hope, then we close down some of the future's possibilities.

2   How can we have hope for our students? It is vital that, regardless of what is going on in our heads, we do not allow negativity to transmit to our students. Too often our systems of targets and measuring can give students a sense that we are limiting what we believe is possible for them. Here Dweck's work on mindsets is significant (see chapter 29).

3   For our colleagues: it is easier to be positive if other people around us are also positive. One sign of a good staffroom is people encouraging each other and praising things they have seen in other classrooms. Be that colleague that gives others hope even if it is not initially returned. Chain reactions have to start somewhere.

Leadership byte

'Lousy leaders use magnifying glasses when things go wrong and wear blindfolds when things go right.'
(Dan Rockwell @leadershipfreak 2016)

How you deal with the successes and failures of your team is vital. When people make mistakes, think about how you can make the conversation supportive so that they are aware of the expectations but also genuinely think that they are able to meet them. Likewise, just as a teacher 'catches children being good' and praises them, make sure you celebrate the successes and you will develop a team that is willing to take more risks in the future.

Yes, but how? Practically speaking

Of course being more positive is easier said than done. This is something we are likely to have ups and downs in. Here are four practical tips:

1 Be mindful. One of the techniques highlighted by Fredrickson is mindfulness. If you are a person of faith, you may practice prayer or meditation already; if not, mindfulness exercises can be useful. Anything where you are able to have a little headspace, as it were, can be a real help in quelling negative thoughts.

2 Create and play. Taking time off work to do something that is creative or just fun can have a similar effect. Journaling or blogging your thoughts can also be beneficial.

3 Keep the positive reminders close at hand. The thank you cards, previous year's results, emails from past students. Remember to 'fix your dashboard' (chapter 10).

4 Avoid people who are overly negative. We do to some extent begin to resemble the company we keep. If there is a member of staff who is constantly complaining, and you don't think they can be helped, a safe distance may be prudent.

? **Questions for reflection**

1 Are there areas in which you have become negative and your focus has narrowed? What possibilities are there that you are currently missing?

2 Have you tried mindfulness techniques or meditation? What other things can you do to get your mind back in balance?

3 Are there people that you need to spend less time with?

Bibliography

Clear, J (2013) *The science of positive thinking: How positive thoughts build your skills, boost your health, and improve your work.* Available from http://www.huffingtonpost.com/james-clear/positive-thinking_b_3512202.html 10/7/13 (Accessed 10th February 2016).

Enyedi, A (2015) *How can teachers avoid burnout?* Available from https://www.britishcouncil.org/voices-magazine/how-can-teachers-avoid-burnout (Accessed 8th February 2016).

Fredrickson, BL, Cohn, MA, Coffey, KA, Pek, J, and Finkel, SM (2008) Open Hearts Build Lives: Positive Emotions, Induced Through Loving-Kindness Meditation, Build Consequential Personal Resources. *Journal of Personality and Social Psychology.* 95(5): 1045–1062.

Reah, M (2014) *Teacher 5 a day.* Available from https://martynreah.wordpress.com/2014/12/06/teacher5aday (Accessed 10th January 2016).

Rockwell, D @leadershipfreak (2016) Available from https://twitter.com/leadershipfreak/status/695951853536747520 (accessed 31st May 2016).

Shaw, GB (1949) *Selected Plays with Prefaces*, New York: Dodd, Mead.

Chapter 21

Shabbat – the importance of rest

It is Friday evening in a traditional Jewish household. After a busy day for all, the woman of the house lights the Sabbath candles, a meal is taken together and work ceases. The Sabbath (Shabbat) runs from Friday sunset until sunset the next day. What this exactly means varies from household to household. For orthodox Jews this may mean no electricity, no cooking and a limit on where and how you may travel. The Saturday will be spent resting with the family; there is likely to be a visit to the synagogue.

As an RE teacher I have always had an admiration for the idea of Shabbat. The exact rules don't really bother me; I am always more interested in principles than rules. What is admirable about Shabbat is the notion of switching off, disconnecting and intentionally engaging in a period of rest. We live in a 24/7 non-stop society. Part of the modern condition that afflicts everyone, not just teachers, is that we never truly disconnect. For teachers, with our open ended contracts and impossible workload, it can be a challenge to take time off. We are always available by email; we are always on Twitter. We are always partially working. This means that when we are at home with our family, we are often not fully there. Yet if we are to survive as teachers and flourish as people, including preparing students for a connected working life, we need to figure out how to switch off. This chapter looks at how we can restore our energy by 'religiously' practicing the idea of Shabbat!

Philosophy corner: the three purposes of Shabbat

Traditionally the Sabbath marks the belief that God created the world in 6 days and rested on the seventh. Of course it is unlikely that an all powerful God rested because he was tired! The Sabbath was given as an example and pattern for humans to follow. It has three main purposes:

1 Rest – This one shouldn't need explaining.

2 Family – The Shabbat is a family occasion, particularly in Judaism, where the family home is arguably more important than the synagogue.

3 Worship – Whether we are 'religious' or not, we are all spiritual and need time to connect and reflect.

Shabbat applied

The ideas of Shabbat, particularly that of rest, can be applied in a number of ways:

1 **Ourselves** – It also goes without saying that, as teachers, we have to be able to switch off. You may or may not have spiritual inclinations, but there is something about resting and reconnecting with your purpose. One of the big dangers in education at the moment is people being too busy to remember why they are doing what they are doing in the first place. There is also something about the importance of rest in enabling greater creativity; it is important that we have some head space in which to solve problems. In the same way that a computer 'defrags' its hard drive periodically and runs more efficiently, so too a mind that is rested tends to make better decisions.

2 **Family** – Even more importantly, it is vital in our family roles that we have some space to be spouses, partners, parents, children of elderly parents. Too often in term time we can be guilty of giving our nearest and dearest the crumbs that fall from our table. There is the phenomenon of absent presence: we sit in the same room at

home, but we are miles away, either working or pondering on some issue at work. The intentional rest 'forces' us to be present at home.

3   **Students** – As leaders in our classrooms, particularly with older students, we need to model and encourage the principle of Shabbat in the young people we teach. I am generally an enthusiast for technology in education, but one of the downsides is that often our young people are incapable of switching off. When I do revision timetables with my A level students, I make a point of encouraging a day off. When a student emails me work at 2 a.m. or on Sunday evening, whereas previously I would email back within minutes or at 6 a.m. the next morning, I now wait until a reasonable hour or even until Monday morning. I am trying to model and lead by example. We need to have conversations with students about switching off – particularly switching off digitally.

4   **Sabbatical** – On the subject of Sabbaths, and being a bit cheeky, there is one policy that, were I to be Secretary of State for education, I would seek to bring in as soon as possible: a paid sabbatical for each teacher of a term every 10 years. I have seen the benefits of sabbaticals in other professions, particularly friends and relatives who are in ministry. People get jaded and burnt out in teaching; good teachers leave. Imagine what a term to reflect, research, visit other institutions, get industry experience or update knowledge could do to transform and renew tired staff. It may not cost as much as we think if these staff return reenergised rather than just leaving teaching.

I suspect that paid sabbaticals are somewhat of a pipe dream; we don't have enough teachers, let alone any spare ones to cover such an idea. But it is not unrealistic for each of us to have some form of weekly Sabbath to restore our energy levels before the next week begins; that includes switching off Twitter!

Yes, but how? Practically speaking

In my week there are probably two Sabbaths rather than one. No matter how busy I am, I will do my best to take one midweek evening off. This is a day when I leave college as close to on-time as I can and do no work that evening. This year, with a full teaching day on Thursday,

Wednesday evening has generally been the midweek Sabbath. The second and more significant Sabbath is at the weekend. At least one of the weekend days will typically be work free – sometimes Saturday, sometimes Sunday, depending on other commitments.

One tip for helping switch the mind from work mode to rest mode is given by Bill Hybels (2008). In a job that is never ending, it is important that we 'create our own finishing lines'. We have a set time that we clock off, as it were, and have a clocking off ritual. This might be 5 minutes tidying our desks each evening before leaving or, on a Friday afternoon, 15 minutes planning and organising our next week's schedules (chapter 33). This tells our minds that the week is over.

? **Questions for reflection**

1 When you are planning ahead, do you build in planned time to rest or does work gradually invade these times?

2 Do you have a midweek evening off? Which evening would be easiest? Which evening would make most sense given your timetable?

Bibliography

Hybels, B (2008) *Axiom – Powerful Leadership Proverbs*, Zondervan: Michigan.

Chapter 22

Let's do lunch

Scenario

Sam is a young, conscientious teacher. In addition to after school revision classes, she runs a lunchtime club one day a week. On those days it is not unusual for Sam to get to 3:30 p.m. and discover that she has not eaten since breakfast. On another day one week, she is invited to a 'working lunch' by a senior manager who is keen to get staff ideas on an aspect of policy. Having eaten half a sandwich and a piece of quiche, she races down the corridor so as not to be late for her first lesson after lunch. Reflecting later in the day, she realises that not only do SLT members never come into the staffroom at lunch, but she had never even seen one of them eat anything.

Sam's case is not unusual. The Aviva Healthcare workplace study in 2011 reported that around 1 in 3 employees nationally regularly skip lunch breaks. Anne Fisher's 2012 article on American office culture suggests that 80% of workers take lunch at their desks. Although exact data for teachers is difficult to obtain, it is not unreasonable to think that the situation is similar or worse. This is often not helped by colleagues who tell callers to 'ring back at 12:30 as he is on lunch then'. The exact opposite of how every other industry and profession operates!

For those staff with really long memories, the 1980s teacher strikes were about the right to have a proper lunch break. We now have our lunch break built into our contract. The downside is that the lunch break is not included in the 1,265 hours. Thus the very phrase a 'working lunch' is an oxymoron. This chapter makes the case that the lunch break is a vital part of sustaining our physical and mental energies. We work through it at our peril.

The case against lunch

Of course there are always good reasons not to take a lunch break:

1   You are keen to run an activity for students. Perhaps running catch up sessions or maybe this is the best time to impose that detention. Ask yourself if this really is the best time and, if so, does it need all of the lunch break?

2   Other colleagues are missing lunch or eating at their desks whilst checking emails. You do not wish to appear uncommitted. As with Sam, the example of the senior team in your school may lead you into thinking that a sandwich at your desk is more professional.

3   You have an optimistic view that if you do half an hour at lunchtime, you will be able to finish earlier tonight. Of course you will only really know if this is the case by having a few days where you do take lunch and then comparing the data!

In my early career I was one of those teachers who regularly gave up lunch but I started to find that my afternoon lessons suffered as a result. Also – although I can't prove it, I'm pretty sure my administrative efficiency was also diminished. Hence I took a decision to take a lunch break each day.

The case for the lunch break

1   It's actually healthier to take a break. Working straight through without a break may be fine in the short term on occasions, but there are cumulative effects on health in the long term if we don't take breaks. According to numerous surveys, our wellbeing is linked to taking breaks.

2   It's more productive. You will work better after a break. We've always got loads to do, but will we honestly get everything done if

we work the extra 30 minutes at lunch? Tony Schwartz – head of the New York based 'Energy Project', who is quoted in the Anne Fisher article (2012) – argues that there is a clear link between exhausted employees not taking breaks and poor performance and burnout.

3   It relieves stress. The ability to sit and chat socially with colleagues about work and life outside it is very cathartic. You will become more relaxed. Many of the most interesting conversations I have had about teaching and learning have occurred over a sandwich in the staffroom.

4   It safeguards the rights we currently have. It's a hard earned right. No one is currently proposing to take it away. The only people that prevent us taking lunch are ourselves. We can't blame managers for this one. Although money certainly isn't everything, if we work through lunch, we are working for free. You are entitled to take lunch. Bear that in mind the next time someone asks you to come to that strange oxymoron – the working lunch.

5   Hygiene – Desks and keyboards often have alarmingly high levels of bacteria – in some cases, even more than toilet seats. To make matters worse, food dropped onto computer keyboards can actually feed these bacteria. So you may be consuming more than you bargained for if you choose to eat at your desk. In a shared office or workroom, there is nothing worse than having to wipe away grease and crumbs before commencing work.

Of course if you feel you must run some sort of lunchtime activity, consider scheduling it for a day where you are not teaching in the lesson before or after lunch. That way you can still have some sort of break.

Leadership byte

Be aware that your teaching staff have full timetables; they are not able to adjust their schedules and give themselves 'space to think and breathe' in the way that a senior colleague with a reduced timetable can. The 30 minutes at lunch may be the only pause in a hectic 9–10 hour day for many staff (see chapter 34). Don't insist or pressure staff to surrender it. Where staff put pressure on themselves, you can alleviate it by being a visible example and taking lunch.

Recently I became aware of the situation of an acquaintance who is a nursery nurse. She is not paid for her lunch hour, but is required by her employers to remain on site and can be called into a room if there is an issue. (And there often is!) She is trying to join a union, but her employers are not impressed. We are in a relatively privileged position as teachers. We are absolutely FREE to take lunch. Of course we may say that we have a culture in which staff do not take breaks, but culture just describes how people currently behave; culture is something that we can change if we so choose. I know it's brave, but why not step away from the computer and let the telephone ring? Try it as an experiment for a week. Let's do lunch!

? Questions for reflection

1 What do you currently do for lunch? Is it a break or is it spent at a PC or in a place where students can interrupt? How well rested are you when you begin the afternoon?

2 What are the main reasons for missing lunch? Peer pressure? Workload? Is missing lunch working for you or not?

Bibliography

Aviva Healthcare (2011) *One in three likely to skip lunch break.* Aviva 'Health of the Workplace' report. Available from https://www.aviva.co.uk/media-centre/story/12663/one-in-three-likely-to-skip-lunch-breaks/ (Accessed 14th February 2016).

Fisher, A (2012) *The case for taking a real lunch break.* Available from http://fortune.com/2012/11/08/the-case-for-taking-a-real-lunch-break/ (Accessed 12th March 2016).

Chapter 23

Surviving holidays – withdrawal symptoms

According to the old joke, October is the month where the cricket fan discovers that his wife left him in August. Only when the season has ended does anything from normal life come to his attention. The grain of truth in this for teachers is that it is not unusual to get to the holiday and feel that reconnecting with life is a bit of a strain. A recent speech given by John Tomsett at a conference likened teaching to being in a submarine: you submerge for 7 weeks or so and then come up for air for a week. This chapter looks at how we come up for air and make the most of what our friends tell us are very generous holidays.

Those holiday feelings

Holidays are meant to be enjoyed not endured. They are one of the benefits of our job. However, holidays bring a change of pace. This is true in all walks of life yet particularly in teaching. There seem to be two main things that prevent teachers from enjoying holidays:

1   **Coming down – the change of pace** – Teaching is in some ways a performance. It can be emotionally draining, and the first day or so of a holiday I can only compare to the feeling of coming off stage. My musical career never really took off, but I was lucky enough to play a few sets opening for bands with real talent. It's a feeling of elation, and you come off stage buzzing but exhausted. Although perhaps not a great analogy, there is something akin to a 'coming down' that happens at the end of a busy term. This changing of

115

pace can equally be a problem on the first day of term when we find ourselves shattered by the exertions of the day. So too at the start of a holiday, the switch from the fast pace of endless things to do to a full stop can be quite disorienting.

2   **Guilt** – Teachers will be quick to tell you that they don't really have long holidays; they have to work to prepare for the next term. One of the difficulties we face is that whilst the work for next term still sits unprepared, we never totally switch off. We have recurring guilt, or we may do an hour or so here and there if we're at home. The age of e-mail and remote access computers compounds the problem. Others may even add to the guilt by asking when in the holiday we will be coming in to support Year 11.

Enjoying your break

In writing this, I am aware that I am very much a work in progress in this area. Hopefully you can learn from my mistakes by doing the following:

1   **Plan your break**. We are busy, and it is very easy for a holiday to arrive and for us to find that we have no real plan about how we are going to use it. It is important that in the last couple of weeks you arrange to see friends, book trips etc. First, this gives us something to look forward to. Second, and perhaps more importantly, it avoids us leaving school on Friday thinking, 'What now?' This lack of purpose or direction and the anxiety that goes with it is known as Existential Angst by philosophers.

2   **Do nothing whilst tired**. Enjoy your rest on the Friday evening and possibly the Saturday. It's YOUR time. You do not HAVE to do anything if you don't want to. Incidentally, never start DIY on the first day of a holiday. Been there, broke that! Listen to your emotional states.

3   **Decide when you're working and stick to it**. Most holidays, I tend to work for a couple of days usually near the start of the break to get it out of the way, but sometimes it's towards the end. If I've planned to leave it till the end, then I don't tend to feel guilty

because I've made a decision to do it then. The vague 'I will do lots of work at some point' is a recipe for recurring guilt; fix the boundaries of your work time. Also try to do work that you enjoy rather than admin or marking.

4   **Know when to stop.** There's always more we can do, but decide how long you are going to spend on work and stick to it. You need to be fresh for the start of the next term.

5   **Invest in yourself and your significant others.** During a busy term, we can often neglect those around us and be too busy to pursue the things we're interested in. This is your time now. Play with the children, read a book, go out for a meal. Invest in your relationships and stimulate your interests. You've worked hard. You deserve it.

Gardening leave

One bizarre side effect of a holiday and putting the brain in rest mode is that you can have more creative thoughts; some of these will relate to work. Sometimes when I am gardening or washing up the solutions to problems at work, such as the way to teach a difficult topic etc. will present themselves. In order to prevent this from sending us back into work mode, why not have a notebook or note app on your tablet where you write these random thoughts? This will prevent you from losing the thought and prevent the thought from disrupting your holiday further. One perk of our job as teachers is reasonably regular 'gardening leave'. It is important that whether we have a literal garden or not, we take advantage of some time to reflect. What issues are there in our teaching, our careers, our families that we need to reflect upon and address? Often the solutions appear when we are not really looking!

Finally – just stop feeling so guilty!

Remember that the holidays are quite generous, but they are not unreasonably so if you are working at least 50 hours a week for three quarters of the year. You will have done at least 1–2 extra unpaid weeks for every 6 that you work. It is not wrong to claim the time back.

? **Questions for reflection**

1 What would you like to do during the next holiday? Is it arranged? Is your summer holiday booked yet?

2 What work will you need to do in preparation for the next term? Will you do this at the start of the holiday or at the end? It is important to decide rather than merely letting it happen.

Chapter 24

Tides, treasure and nudity – managing change

The scene is a staff meeting at Anytown Comprehensive (soon to become 'Shiny Heights Academy'):

Head: Which brings me to our next item – this is a new government policy and there's going to be a new whole school initiative on this.

Teacher: Great; it's been a while since the last initiative. Thursday, wasn't it?

Head: Well, quite. I'm pleased you've taken it so well; I have to say I was expecting some resistance.

Teacher: Not at all. I'm delighting that initiative 26 has been replaced by this scheme which so clearly works. It does work, doesn't it? This is proven to raise achievement, right?

Head: Well, Ofsted seem to think so – and how often are they wrong? I expect there's some study or other.

Teacher: So initiative 26 is redundant, isn't it?

Head: I'm not sure – Clearly, initiative 27 is very different in tone, has a different nuance in places and has two direct contradictions with many aspects of initiative 26; however, the government haven't actually said, and they may well bring together both elements in initiative 28 or 29 next week.

Teacher: Well, on a positive note – I think this will cut down some of the paperwork and allow me to focus on what happens in the classroom.

Head: Interesting, not really thought of it that way.

Teacher: I was being sarcastic!

Variations on this scene are played out regularly in every school and college in the country. Everything constantly changes. Numerous things change each year; by the time results improve or decline, there are so many variables that it is impossible to confidently say which has led to the improvement (or decline). This chapter considers the energy required to manage change and how we understand the emotional journey that change brings.

Types of change

Most changes seem to bring more work and unfortunately that work is not always directly related to what happens with students in the classroom. One of the great skills of surviving in teaching is to navigate these changes and engage with them with the enthusiasm (or apathy!) that they deserve. There are a number of different types of initiatives and changes, and each requires a different technique:

1   **The Emperor's clothes – the useless.** We all know the story of the emperor's new clothes. They aren't clothes at all. In fact the emperor is naked. Similarly many new ideas are precisely that. On reflection, and often after the event, we see that the initiative/policy/change was pointless. We may all have suspected it but lacked the courage to openly say so. That was my experience on one occasion when a senior manager said to me discreetly that only one person in the building genuinely believed this particular idea – unfortunately, it was the headteacher! One of the great frustrations of such initiatives is that we are frequently caught between two stools – lacking the guts to dispense with the idea completely but also lacking belief in its value – so we approach it half-heartedly and treat it as a pointless tick box exercise. This is the worst of all options as it then both costs time and fails to deliver results. Things should either be done properly or not at all.

2   **Canute's tide – the inevitable.** Alternatively, there are things that can't be ignored. Sometimes we make the wrong call about new

ideas. Many a teacher 20 years ago expressed the view that ICT was a passing fad, but those who have ignored it have done so at their peril. Like King Canute, we need to be aware that there are certain things that we cannot control and have to accept. In fact they may positively improve the work we do with our students. There are some ideas and initiatives that we simply must engage with and if we must do something, then we might as well try to do it properly. We may have severe misgivings about exam specification changes, but there may well be nothing we can do. Some ideas are like tides; we have to metaphorically get a surfboard and ride the wave.

3　**The Staffordshire hoard – the hidden gem.** Equally, in Staffordshire, we are well aware of the story of the treasure that is the Staffordshire hoard. The story goes that a farmer in quite an ordinary field began to discover treasure with his metal detector. Of course, it could so easily have remained undiscovered. For us in education it's easy to approach a training session or staff meeting with weariness – it's 'just another field'. Maybe that attitude prevents us from seeing the treasure and the possibilities offered. If we approach things positively and with an open mind, we may end up pleasantly surprised. There's 'treasure' here – some ideas that may actually work, a better way of doing what we're doing. So keep an open mind.

Of course it is often quite difficult to know the difference. This is where it is really important to keep up our reading of educational articles in magazines, blogs or in books. It will help us to sort the ideas into the three categories above. If we have decided that the change in question is either compulsory or desirable – it will bring benefits to our students – then we just have to do our best by planning ahead so that we manage the change well.

Unfortunately deciding which horse to back, as it were, is not an exact science because education, and anything in which you are dealing with people, is not an exact science. In a world that craves certainty and demands that strategies are implemented mechanically and without flexibility, perhaps the teacher is more like artist than scientist, using a range of techniques to suit the occasion and audience.

It is important to be open to change and new ideas, but each of us has to decide how they apply in our particular situations.

'Life is a rollercoaster' – riding the change curve

The change curve (Diagram 24.1) was first identified by Elizabeth Kubler Ross to describe the recovery of patients following surgery (Oakes and Griffin, 2013). It is not unusual to experience similar emotions when we undergo significant change in the workplace. As people we prefer familiarity and patterns; we can find change disconcerting. Having gone through significant changes and attempted to lead change as a lead practitioner for ILT, I have noticed that there is certainly some truth in this. It is important that we are aware that change can be psychologically stressful and that we challenge negative thoughts when they manifest themselves. This is worth bearing in mind if you are in leadership and are introducing necessary changes. Be aware that change is stressful; challenge emotions, and if you are in leadership, watch out for the emotions of others.

Diagram 24.1 The Change Curve

Used with permission: © A Level Mindset, Oakes, S. & Griffin, M (2013). http://www. alevelmindset.com/#!Making-the-jump-from-GCSE-to-A-Levels/c21x0/1 Diagram used with permission.

? Questions for reflection

1 Consider some of the current changes you are dealing with. Are they things you have to do? Will they benefit students? If the answer to either of those questions is yes, how will you bring it about? Plan ahead.

2 What guidance or directives do you need to avoid? How will you distinguish the difference between the useful and the useless? What do you do to keep up to date?

Bibliography

Oakes, S and Griffin, M (2013) *Making the jump from GCSE to A Levels.* Available from http://www.alevelmindset.com/#!Making-the-jump-from-GCSE-to-A-Levels/c21xo/1 (Accessed 12th March 2016).

Chapter 25

Just say 'no'

We have all been there: a well-meaning colleague comes to us at a time convenient to them yet inconvenient to us. It may be as we are scurrying down a corridor towards our next lesson or, more often than not, as we are entering the toilet! Perhaps we are entering or leaving the building and our brain isn't totally in work mode. The request sounds harmless enough and tends to begin with the three words 'can you just . . .?' 'Can you just look at the data for the year 11 classes and identify which students need further intervention?' 'Can you just look at the RE planning for key stage one in the summer term and build in some more kinaesthetic tasks?'

It is important that we are aware of the word 'just'; its slips in there and implies that what we are being asked to do is straightforward and is no big thing. Yet this may or may not be the case. One way to test this is to imagine whether they would still use the word 'just' if you just happened not to do it! This chapter looks at how and when we might need to say no. Saying this short word is a vital skill to learn. If we are to maintain our energy levels in the long term it will not be possible to say yes all the time.

Why do we find it so hard to say no?

There are several reasons that teachers find it tough to say no:

1   'Yes' is quicker – given that many of these requests are hurried conversations when we have other things to do, 'yes' gets us out of the conversation quicker than a 'no' or a 'maybe'.

2 Desire to please – as was mentioned earlier, most teachers were successful at school themselves by being compliant and enjoying the praise of our teachers. We don't want to upset people, particularly those in authority.

3 Desire to get ahead – we realise, particularly when an additional responsibility is being offered, that if we decline then someone else may be offered the opportunity and they may get ahead of us. One of the more unpleasant aspects of current performance management systems is that they seem to have introduced an unhealthy type of competition into the staffroom.

4 We don't want to be the one that lets the team down – we are pretty sure that everyone else is saying yes.

When yes ends up being no

Whilst 'yes' may be easier and helps avoid embarrassment or awkwardness, it is very easy for our 'yes' to end up becoming 'no' by default. If we say yes to everything that we are asked to do, then we are presented with a difficulty: either we do everything and, in doing so, do everything superficially and badly, or we end up failing to do something else that is on our list. Worse still is when we don't actually do the thing we have said that we will do; in our desire to show ourselves to be responsible and efficient, we manage to project the opposite!

Saying yes hastily causes a twofold problem: first, our energy becomes divided even further; we do not give our students or our family the time and energy that they need. We can find ourselves trying to do something important when we are tired. Second, we can lose sense of focus and purpose. The fourth section of this book deals with the importance of a clear focus. As well as energy, we only have a finite amount of attention; focus on too many different things at once and something is likely to escape your vision.

Saying no: when and how

Of course there are times when you are unable to say no for very legitimate reasons: the situation is genuinely urgent, the request is something that will lead to a greater good, or it is something that you actually want to do. There are also times when there is no point saying no, as the request is regarding something inevitable. Yet at other times, saying no is a possibility. However, it can be quite a challenge, and it is important that we consider ways of doing this tactfully but firmly. The following suggestions may help:

1   **Hit the pause button.** Buy yourself some thinking time especially if the request has come out of the blue. 'Can I get back to you later on this as I am currently . . .?' Explain that you are about to teach or have some essential admin to get in. Tell them when you will get back to them and stick to it. Hitting the pause button on such conversations means that if you say yes, you know that you can genuinely commit and, if you say no, you will able to explain your reasoning more clearly. Either way, you come across as a reflective and thoughtful professional.

2   **Not now** . . . Similar to the above, explaining that now is not a good time but you will be able to do the task next week or that your situation may be different in a few months' time regarding the extra responsibility means that you are not giving an outright 'no'; the door is left ajar, and if they are willing to wait, your 'no' will become a 'yes'. If they are not willing to wait, that is their choice, not yours.

3   **I have already** . . . Sometimes requests, particularly those involving admin, seem to duplicate things that we have already done. Be brave and ask whether what has already been done is enough. 'My tracking isn't on the spreadsheet, but we have our own tracker on Google docs. Can I share that with you?' If the work you have already done is effectively the same thing as what is being asked, only a particularly callous or dim manager would expect you to duplicate work.

4   **My current priorities are** . . . 'I would love to but I'm unable as I am currently focusing on . . .' Explain what your priorities are for the week or the half term; they are such that you would be unable to do justice to what you're being asked to do. Ask if they agree that those priorities are important.

5   **I'm concerned that my students** . . . Allied to number 4 is an appeal to the negative impact upon the students. As a teacher your

primary job is to plan, teach and mark. Express your concern if you feel that the request will distract you from the job of teaching. This is particularly so when asked to do data analysis (see the section in chapter 28 titled 'Eyes on the Ball Not on the Scoreboard'). Again it would take a brave or stupid manager to ask you to prioritise something that harms students.

Whichever of the above you take – and you may even have a stock phrase of your own – try to put the ball back in the other person's court. You can do this by offering a choice: I could do a rough attempt at this now but would do a better job next term when the exam classes have left; which do they prefer? Often by delaying and inviting them to come back to you at a later date, situations take care of themselves. It is not unusual for some of these urgent requests to end up not being too important after all.

Yes, but how? Practically speaking

Many of us find saying no quite difficult. Although it may seem a little cheesy, practice saying no either with a trusted friend/partner or on your own in front of the mirror. Aim to find the right balance between assertive and polite. If you have rehearsed the lines a few times, it will be easier to deliver the lines the next time you are onstage.

? Questions for reflection

1 We often have a tendency to be 'yes people'. What pressures or personality traits might cause you to say yes when no would be a better answer?

2 What are your current priorities? How would an additional task or responsibility sit with them?

3 What strategies can you use to say 'no' without being impolite or appearing unprofessional?

Chapter 26

Voice – looking after your number one tool

Our voices are our livelihood. Most of us are using our voices between 20 and 25 hours each week, and despite our best efforts we will inevitably do some of this at a higher volume or pitch than we would like. Begin to type the words 'voice care' into Google and the top suggestion is 'voice care for teachers.' Yet apart from a few pages of tips on some of the union websites, there is relatively little from within education on how to look after our number one tool.

This is in stark contrast to other performance roles. Actors and singers performing 2–3 hours a night get vocal coaching and advice on how to look after their voices. When I did finally, after over 15 years as a teacher, manage to get a day with a vocal coach, it was because it had been arranged by my church on the grounds that I might be speaking for 20 minutes or so once a month. When I told her what I did for a living, she duly rolled her eyes and explained that teachers had lots of vocal problems. This seems to be supported by claims on various union websites that suggest teachers can be up to 8 times more likely than the rest of the population to develop issues with their voices.

Hopefully one day vocal workshops will become part of initial teacher training, topped up with a couple of hours on an INSET day every few years. Until then this chapter looks at what we can do in the classroom and beyond to help avoid vocal problems developing.

Your voice in the classroom

When we reflect on how we use our voice in the classroom, it is of course obvious to us that we are speaking too much, too loudly and probably at too high a pitch. A number of the following suggestions may seem to be common sense but they are easily forgotten in the heat of battle, so to speak:

1   Pitch – Think carefully about the pitch of your voice. Although there is debate about the legitimacy of the following terms, your pitch can be divided into chest voice, mixed voice and head voice. These depend on where the vibrations are when you speak. Try relaxing and humming a note without thinking, and then place your hands on your upper chest and jaw to feel where the vibrations are. If they are just below the throat, that is chest voice; if you feel vibrations at both throat and jaw, that's mixed voice; and if you feel them at the jaw (mouth/face), that's head voice. This should give you the pitch that is most natural to you. Aim to use this pitch most often. Some of us, myself included, have a tendency to use a higher pitched, unnatural head voice a little more than we need to. In doing so we can inadvertently strain our voices.

2   Volume – Excessive shouting is bad for your voice. Equally we can be guilty of being louder than we need to be in order to reach the back of the room. Sue Cowley's claim that we are talking too loudly for around 90% of the time in class does not seem widely off the mark (2009, p. 47). Quiet down so that they need to listen to hear. Often the noise level and fidgeting of the class is a direct response to our volume levels. If you absolutely must shout, do so from the diaphragm not the throat and reduce your volume immediately once you have gained attention. If you do feel the need to reprimand the class, doing so in a quiet and measured voice can be more sinister. Sustained shouting just damages the voice and provides amusement for some classes.

3   Reduce your words – Aim to get whole class instructions or explanations down to the absolute minimum. Like me, you might be guilty of over-explaining. If you find yourself regularly beginning

sentences with the words 'to repeat . . .' or 'another way of saying this is . . .', then consider whether these could be cut. You have plenty of other ways to check whether students have understood.

4 The sound of silence – Use non-verbal classroom management techniques where possible. The silent stare or scowl at the chatterer, the arms folded in front of the room or having a pre-arranged signal such as the raised hand where you want silence can all work to good effect. Requests to listen, put something away, or to turn around can also be conveyed by miming the action in question. Such strategies are effective in achieving the aims of saving your voice, getting a student on task and helping students not lose face in front of peers.

5 Use the space – Don't be afraid to move around the room. It shows confidence that all of the room is your territory; it may also save your voice. Whispering 1–1 next to the student in question is far better than calling across the room, both in terms of classroom management and your voice. You can also teach from any part of the room – perhaps right next to the student who is prone to wander off task. Get a 'clicker' to help you do this. You do not have to be chained to your PC. Move around.

Finally, if you are teaching all day, remember to **drink plenty of water**.

Troubleshooting – your voice outside the classroom

If you were a singer or theatre actor you would do vocal warm-ups prior to going onstage, yet as teachers we tend to get out of the car, have a coffee, sort our resources and go straight on stage, exerting our voice. Whilst vocal warm up sessions in the staffroom may make us feel a tad self-conscious, there is no reason why we can't sing along to a song in the car or hum a scale or two on the way to the classroom.

Likewise at the end of the day a period of silence to allow the vocal cords to recover would be the equivalent of the opera singer not speaking for a day after a concert. Building in regular periods of quiet not only helps your voice but also does wonders for your general wellbeing.

Of course there is some bad news. Mucus is your enemy when it comes to looking after your throat and voice. This means that foods such as milk and cheese, as well as drinks such as tea and coffee and wine, can add to any problems you have by increasing mucus. Smoking also dries out the vocal chords (if you are looking for yet another reason to stop).

If your voice is struggling, various remedies are suggested: gargling with salt water, honey, mouthwashes, and my personal favourite, steam. If you happen to have a gym membership and your gym has a steam room, this can do wonders for your breathing and vocal chords.

And finally, even when you are not in the classroom, one of the best ways of looking after your voice is to remember to **drink lots of water**.

Long term voice care

It is tempting to carry on if your voice is struggling. I have certainly seen a few teachers in my time controlling a class on a hoarse whisper and some charades. However, if we are serious about our voices, we need to be off work and resting it even if we feel physically well otherwise. If your voice does not return after 2–3 days, that is the time when you need to get medical advice. If there are long term issues then occupational health should be involved, and if you are likely to need a microphone in order to prevent further damage, then they should provide one. Hopefully it shouldn't get to that stage.

Finally, just **drink loads of water**!

? **Questions for reflection**

1 Have you had issues with your voice during your career? If so, what do you think was the cause of it? What may have made it worse?

2 Do you talk too much or too loudly in class? What could you do to improve your non-verbal classroom management skills?

3 Are you drinking enough water? Are you also drinking or consuming things that are bad for your throat?

Bibliography

ATL (2016) *Voice care*. ATL website. Available from https://www.atl.org.uk/health-and-safety/staff-and-pupil-issues/voice-care.asp (Accessed 14th February 2016).

Cowley, S (2009) *Teaching Skills for Dummies*, Chichester: John Wiley & Sons.

Lee, K (2013) *4 ways to look after your voice*. Available from http://www.katelee.co.uk/blog/4-ways-to-look-after-your-voice/ (Accessed 14th February 2016).

Part 4

Focus

Chapter 27

Distractions – keeping the main thing the main thing

According to social commentator Phil Cooke in *Jolt*, 'For better or worse, disruption is the word that best describes 21st century living' (2011, p. xiii). As teachers we face the disruption of change on a constant basis. There are new technologies, new strategies, and new government policies. Each of these changes causes a disruption – a jolt – to our way of working.

On a more mundane level, as we come into work armed with our list of things to do, we experience the disruption of e-mail, the ringing of the phone, the knocks on the workroom door, the conversation with a colleague that reminds you of something you haven't done. All of these disturb our working day. Our job as teachers is complex in terms of the variables and interactions, yet relatively simple in terms of its core aim. We mark, we plan, we teach and repeat (Morrison McGill 2015, p. 5). Yet life is not that simple, and the things listed above can distract and overwhelm us. This section looks at keeping focus and perspective and, in particular in this chapter, how we keep the main thing as the main thing.

One job or two?

In some ways the job of teaching is in reality two separate jobs. First there is the job of being in a classroom and working with students. This is your job for around 20 hours each week. Then there is the office job: the planning, marking, administration and organisation that go with teaching, especially if you have any management responsibility. The workload diary and other studies suggest that this can be an additional 30–40 hours each week. On any given day, an unsorted 'things to do' list can have between 15 and 20 things on it. One tool that I have found useful in sorting the 'office job' is the Covey quadrant. It helps me to sort tasks, do one at a time and, crucially, not panic!

Introducing the Covey quadrant

Table 27.1 The Covey Quadrant

	Urgent	Non-urgent
Important	I	II
Not important	III	IV

Table 27.1 is the Covey time management quadrant made famous by Stephen Covey, although sometimes Eisenhower gets the credit. You may have come across it if you have done any sort of leadership course. Although I had been aware of it for several years, it is only in the last couple of years that I have started to use it. It has proved really useful in helping me to notice just where my time is going and to do the job better.

Box I: important and urgent

In this box, I place a 'standing order'. It says simply 'planning'. Every day and every week, this is job number one. As well as day to day planning of lessons, this includes a weekly: 'When do I need ICT facilities?' 'What needs to go in for photocopying?' No matter what other roles we have, this is our first priority. If we do it well, we will feel good about our work as a whole; do it badly and no amount of smooth administration will compensate. Bonus tip: do not get sucked into admin whilst you are teaching. Turn off the emails and leave the spreadsheets in the office. Aim to focus fully in class.

Joining planning in box I in any given week can be a variety of things. In recent weeks, chasing up non-completion of work and non-attenders, marking of mock exams, and analysis of late exam re-marks have all made box I. Some weeks, we will barely make it out of box I, but no matter – we can be pretty confident we are focusing on what matters.

Box II: important but not urgent (aka the strategic)

Perhaps the most vital lesson learned is that box II comes before box III: there are often things that are strategic and important for long term success and wellbeing, but these may not be the things that people are currently screaming at you for. In this box goes forward planning for events, organising of electronic resources on the VLE for revision, the preparation for a new specification. These are future focused things that I need to get moving on that will benefit me and hopefully the college at a later date.

Box III: urgent but not important (aka the distractions)

As stated earlier, one of the curses of modern working life is the constant interruption. This is certainly the case in teaching, as the emails land, the phone rings, a new form to fill in is found or someone appears with 'Can I just have a word about . . .' Occasionally some of these interruptions are box I or II level, but mostly they can be dealt with later. For instance you can arrange to meet that student at another time when convenient to you. And finally here is something to consider: if you find that some of your marking goes into box III (not box I), could you be setting unnecessary tasks? Why set work that is unimportant? Our time and that of our students is precious.

Box IV: non-urgent non-important task

Into box IV go things that it might be nice to do, such as change a display, or things that we are asked to do that seem useless. If you are like me, you will rarely get to anything that you have put into this box. We are too busy. Things will either naturally migrate into another box or can be gradually forgotten. There have been several pieces of pointless admin in the last couple of years that I have correctly guessed were pointless and would not be revisited. By putting them into box IV, much time has been saved.

As a final observation, of course the boxes are quite fluid, and sometimes items move! The tasks get put into the quadrant at the start of the week, but 2–3 minutes at the end of each day (asking 'What do I need to take home?') and 2–3 minutes in the morning (planning what will be done and when that day) help keep things on track. We may never have an empty desk, and we won't always get it right, but the quadrant does help!

The distraction of e-mails

E-mail is a particular 'box III' issue that deserves its own section. In *The Tyranny of Email*, John Freeman claims that an average American corporate worker can spend up to 40% of their day sending, receiving or dealing with e-mail. E-mail has been shown to be addictive in the way that slot machines are shown to be addictive (cited in Cooke 2011, p. xiv). There is something satisfying about sending or dealing with several e-mails. We may work with our e-mails kept open and, when the little blue bar raises its head, we probably stop what we are doing and read the message. Hence we have lost our focus on what we were doing.

In a day's teaching, e-mail and other such disruptions can be more difficult to deal with. We have several hours where the e-mails keep coming, the things to do list keeps growing and we are not able to do anything about it. That time is called 'lessons'. A little while ago I went off to teach a lesson and came back to find the usual five or six e-mails. Three were from the same person (an official at the exam board); they all had the red flag of importance, and the third one was an update on the first based on the assumption that I was just choosing not to reply! If you are teaching: check email before entering class, possibly at lunchtime and at the end of the day. At other times, leave it alone and focus on what you doing.

One strategy I have adopted for emails is to create a folder in my inbox marked 'deal with me'. I park urgent (but not necessarily

important) e-mails in there so that a) I don't forget about them and
b) they don't disturb what I am currently doing.

Finally . . .

> Teaching is a lifetime's craft. You will never perfect it, nor complete
> your to do list. Accept this early on and you will begin to master the
> art of resilience: know when to stop, when to switch off and when it
> is time to look after you!
>
> (Morrison McGill 2015, p. 42)

Ross Morrison McGill is right that the 'to do' list is never ending. It
can be both addictive and overwhelming. Yet it is important to have
one! Having tasks in the right order and focusing on one at a time is
efficient. If you can achieve most of the things you prioritise, you are
doing very well.

? **Questions for reflection**

1 Do you use the Covey Quadrant or similar tool to organise the
things you need to do? If not, why not?

2 Do you have an email addiction? Could you deal with email more
efficiently than you currently do?

Bibliography

Cooke, P (2011) *Jolt!*, Nashville: Thomas Nelson.
Morrison McGill, R (2015) *Teacher Toolkit: Helping You Survive Your First 5 Years*,
London: Bloomsbury.

Chapter 28

Eyes on the ball not on the scoreboard

Case study

Amy's performance review with the Assistant Head was as expected. He was an efficient humourless man who had coloured spreadsheets for everything. He briefly skirted over the school production which she had successfully organised last summer and the Saturday street dance club that had developed good links in the community. The problem was the GCSE drama group; the A–C's were 10% below target. Amy tried to point him to previous year's results, the excellent feedback on her lesson observations, the strong data on her other classes, the thank you cards. It was no use; the GCSE group had been one of her targets – that GCSE 11 group where three students whom the music teacher refused to teach had been dumped. He informed her that she had not met the criteria for pay progression year. Waiting until she was safely in the staff toilets, she burst into tears. It seemed that all the extra things she had worked so hard on last year had been in vain.

In the public sector we have gone through a period of being obsessed with targets; this obsession in the NHS was spectacularly exposed in the Stafford Hospital scandal, where all manner of boxes were ticked and targets met, yet patients needlessly died. Unfortunately, in many schools and colleges, we are in fact still there in the grip of what

Attwood et al. call a 'mad management virus'. We are in systems where control is top down and it is believed that regular inspection and monitoring of targets is the way to improvement. Of course, when that doesn't work, it is simply because you set the wrong targets or had insufficient targets. This chapter looks at how to retain focus and sanity when working within a target driven culture.

Tails wagging the dogs – where does it all go wrong?

Stories such as Amy's are fairly common, and this is unlikely to change any time soon given the financial climate that schools and colleges operate in. It is important to say that whilst we do need ways of assessing how well we are performing so that we can continue to improve, the ways in which this is done vary considerably between institutions. There are a number of ways things can go wrong:

1   Losing the wood for the trees – The requirement to have a very specific focus risks excluding other things. Just as a hospital cannot claim to have had a good year if it has hit a target on waiting times but the speed of the admission process has led to more deaths, so too we may hit a target for one thing but completely miss something more important because we were not told to look at it. You may well achieve your target of doing group work every lesson, but if that comes at the expense of written practice and lowers results, then it is hardly a cause for celebration.

2   Oversimplification – Although things should be simplified as much as possible, the danger with target setting systems is that they overly simplify the complex. Teaching and learning are complex; broadly speaking, the better they are, the better the results. But other than results, it is difficult to measure! Just as a league table does not always show the best football manager, so too there are other factors that we cannot measure. The things we can measure: how many students got level 5, are learning objectives differentiated, is there a starter activity. These are not always the important things.

3   Forgetting the people – Ultimately targets and performance management are mechanistic; they are based on industrial models and assume that people will always behave in strict, predictable ways. As we saw in part 2 of this book, that is a denial of what it means to be a person.

Hence, although ideally we would like a simple system to measure the complex, the reality is that we create a complex system to measure the simple.

Leadership byte: theory X or theory Y?

As a thought experiment, imagine what the difference would be if there were no targets, no performance management and no accountability measures such as league tables. The key issue here is motivation. Performance management and targets are based on what McGregor calls theory X management. This is the idea that workers are essentially reluctant and need constant monitoring and direction. Thus appraisals take a carrot and stick approach. Yet most teachers, and arguably most workers, are theory Y people. They take responsibility and pride in their work and are intrinsically motivated. McGregor's claim was that organisations run in a theory Y way are more productive, yet we insist on managing the efficiency of teachers using a punitive theory X model.

Key idea: watch the ball

The key impact in education of endless targets and tables is that they force us to take our eyes off the ball, as it were. The situation we face is not unlike what often happens in cricket. Once a batsman has got going in an inning, two of the more dangerous periods are when his score is in the nineties or just after he has reached a hundred and he relaxes. One theory is that he loses focus and starts to contemplate the scoreboard rather than fully concentrating on the ball. The danger of targets and performance management where they are done badly is that they are incredibly distracting; they force us to focus on the score-board or spreadsheet rather than how we are going to improve things by planning our next lesson thoroughly. To use a sporting proverb: if we are focused on the ball, then the scoreboard will eventually take care of itself.

Targets and tables: making it all go right

Performance reviews and targets are not destructive in every setting. Some schools and colleges are more than making the best of a bad job. One example is cited by John Tomsett at Huntingdon School. He argues that teachers should set themselves (e.g. not have imposed) challenging targets that they may not meet; the review should be broad and focus on whole performance. This includes exam results, lesson observation feedback, work scrutinies and reflections on CPD and anything else that the teacher thinks is important. At Huntingdon 'meeting the objectives is not a prerequisite for a successful review' (Tomsett 2015, p. 132).

Practically speaking, making things go well for us may mean four things:

1   Choose targets wisely – make sure they fit with the direction that your institution and your department are already travelling and are not arbitrary add ons. Take time to read your school's documentation, look at departmental data and think carefully. Get it right and the things you are focusing on will be box I or II from the Covey Quadrant (see chapter 27) and you will hardly notice them as targets – you were doing those things anyway. Get it wrong and they become Covey Quadrant box III items and threaten to distract you from the real work.

2   Make sure there are a manageable number of targets. It may be seen as heroic to have three or four extra targets, but there is a limit to what we can focus on properly. See chapter 32 on 6 by 6 organisation.

3   Plan in times when progress will be monitored. For exam based targets, a week or so after an assessment has been marked may be sensible. Three or four reviews per year are plenty, and using a system such as Google Docs or Dropbox may enable you to have a live document and avoid reduplication of work.

4 Where things are going wrong, speak up early and ask for support. This is not a weakness; it is the sign of a reflective professional. It is better than only noticing there's a problem once the target isn't met.

With regard to performance management, targets and league tables, there is so much that we cannot change. Yet they have a way of persuading us of their importance and forcing us to switch focus. With regard to such things, we have to be a little more sanguine; after all, hitting targets is not what gets us out of bed each morning.

? Questions for reflection

1 Do you know what your targets are? Who chose them and which section of your Covey Quadrant would they go in?

2 Honestly what motivates you? What would you do anyway even if there was no prospect of a pay rise and no system of monitoring?

3 How do you track your progress against targets? Can you be slicker so as not to create extra work? Could you suggest this to your SLT?

Bibliography

Attwood, M, Pedler, M, Pritchard, S and Wilkinson, D (2003) *Leading Change: A Guide to Whole Systems Working*, Bristol: Policy Press.

The Economist (2008, 6 October) *Theories X and Y*. Available from www.economist.com/node/12370445 (Accessed 15th February 2016).

Tomsett, J (2015) *This Much I Know about Love Over Fear*, Camarthen: Crown House.

Chapter 29

Mindset – compliance vs engagement

Sportspeople, their coaches and sports psychologists have known the secret for years. Mental attitude matters to success. In education we are slowly catching up. There have been several lively debates in recent times about mindset, grit, character education, and whether these things are innate or can be taught. Reading Carol Dweck's book *Mindset* (2006), as opposed to the misrepresentation of her work that sometimes occurs in the press, proved enlightening both in terms of thinking about my students and about the role of teacher. This chapter looks at how we can use mindset theory to help us focus on growth and the future rather than having negative thoughts about the past.

Psychology corner: Dweck's mindset theory

In her book *Mindset* (2006), psychology professor Carol Dweck argues that the main key to success in life is what we believe about ourselves. Broadly speaking we fall into two main groups: a fixed mindset group that believes ability is natural and fixed and a growth mindset group that believes that ability can be changed and developed. The view we adopt of ourselves can profoundly affect how we lead our lives. Dweck argues that we can be more successful by choosing/training ourselves to adopt a growth mindset.

Because a fixed mindset believes intelligence, personality and ability are broadly fixed, it tends not to value effort – if you have

---

a talent, you don't need to work at it, and if you don't have it, why bother trying? People with fixed mindsets understand their own ability through comparison to others and find others threatening. They fear getting things wrong, and they prefer praise to a challenge. They take criticism personally rather than seeing it as a chance to develop.

A growth mindset believes intelligence and personality can be developed and cultivated; talents and aptitudes etc. are merely a starting point. People with growth mindsets are 'oriented towards learning' and have a special talent for identifying their own strengths and weaknesses. They understand that hard work and effort can bring big changes in ability and performance. They enjoy difficulty and challenge and see getting things wrong as a useful step towards getting it right.

Mindset and the students

As a sixth form college teacher, I notice the large number of students who come to A Level having done reasonably well by coasting at GCSE. They are ill prepared for effort and assume wrongly that the need for effort means 'they are thick'. Other students, weaker on paper but used to having to work hard, often overtake them during the course of the year. As a department, we have done a lot of work around mindset in induction and, like other schools, are able to cite examples from sport, music and business of determination and effort to pay off.

Another key implication is in terms of praise. Dweck (2006) argues that we should praise effort more than we praise ability. To praise ability constantly reinforces the idea that ability is fixed. Students need to have their effort praised and see that it is their effort that brings results.

We also have to beware false praise. We are encouraged to start with a positive and end with a positive when providing feedback, and there is a tendency in education to soften bad news or mark generously. This lowering of the bar is not helpful in the long term. 'Growth minded teachers tell students the truth and then give them the tools to close the gap' (Dweck 2006, p. 388).

Mindset for teachers – an exercise

One of the key tools that we have used with students is a diagnostic questionnaire. This one in Table 29.1 is adapted from those used by John Tomsett (2013) and Lorraine Abbott (2014). Try answering the questions honestly but without overthinking!

Once you have added up your score and divided by 6, you will have a mean score. Although this not an exact science, if your score is below 4 it may indicate a fixed mindset; if significantly over 4, it suggests a growth mindset. We are no different from our students in that a growth mindset is the better state. The good news is that it is possible to develop and change. Our brains have a plasticity and we can relearn and change our attitudes with work.

Mindset for teachers – what now?

Having initially read Dweck (2006) with a view to implementing the ideas with students, I became aware of some areas of my own thinking that had become negative and fixed over time! The challenge of adopting a growth mindset as teachers comes in several areas:

1   Feedback – Provided feedback is fair, it is helpful in enabling us to improve and become better. However, we rarely welcome it. Partly due to the punitive systems that we sometimes work in, we are more likely to become defensive than take comments on board. As ungraded lesson observations gain more ground, we will, I hope, be more open to reflecting on feedback and considering whether there is truth in what has been said.

2   Future focus – Growth mindset gives us a future focus. Rather than weighing ourselves against our peers, our aim is to grow and develop. Dylan Wiliam's point about teachers improving because they can be even better comes to mind here. We are not static, and those things that we currently can't do may be possible with effort.

3   Engagement not compliance – When we are managed in a very direct and authoritarian way, as seems to be happening in so many schools, a fixed mindset focus on compliance can be the result.

Table 29.1 Diagnostic Questionnaire

Statement	Strongly agree 1	Agree 2	Mostly Agree 3	Mostly Disagree 4	Disagree 5	Strongly Disagree 6
Your intelligence is something basic about you, and you can't change it very much.						
You can learn new things but can't change how intelligent you are.						
You are a certain kind of person; there's not much you can do to change it.						
You can do some things differently, but the important parts of you don't really change.						
Natural ability is more likely to lead to success than just working hard.						
I find negative feedback demotivating; it doesn't help me work any harder.						

After all if we have no control or autonomy, so long as we tick the boxes and do as we are told we can stay out of trouble. However, there is a better way; a growth mindset does not settle for compliance; it seeks engagement. It is important that we begin to take responsibility and ownership of our teaching.

? **Questions for reflection**

1 Which teachers that you have worked with came to mind when you read the chapter? How did they embody a fixed or growth mindset? If you can't think of any teachers, which people do you consider to have a growth mindset? What can you learn from them?

2 Do you think the questionnaire was accurate in revealing your mindset? Are there any areas of your life inside or outside of work where you have become stuck in fixed mindset thinking?

3 Think of a time when you have had negative feedback. Was it fair? How did you respond?

4 Are there aspects of your role in which you need to step up your engagement as opposed to your compliance?

Bibliography

Abbott, L (2014) *My mindset journey* blog. Available from https://lorraineabbott.wordpress.com/2014/05/19/my-mindset-journey/ (Accessed 15th February 2016).

Dweck, CS (2006) *Mindset: How You Can Fulfil Your Potential*, New York: Random House.

Tomsett, J (2013) *This much I know about developing a Dweck-inspired Growth Mindset culture* blog. Available from https://johntomsett.com/2013/10/20/this-much-I-know-about-developing-a-dweck-inspired-growth-mindset-culture/ (Accessed 15th February 2016).

Chapter 30

Keep growing – invest in yourself

In my first year of teaching in the late 1990s, I used chalk on a blackboard. The VHS video player could be booked if I wished, there was one room of computers in the whole building, and the most sophisticated device in my classroom was the overhead projector. As I teach now, most students in my room are on iPads or Chromebooks and sharing documents with me via Google Classroom or Google docs. They can continue learning during and after class by accessing a range of resources on the VLE. Periodically learning is checked via interactive quizzes. To some extent, little has changed: it is still about relationships, communication and subject content; yet in another way, everything is constantly changing. Just as we are preparing students for a world that no-one can fully see, so too the classrooms of the future may be different to what we imagine. As teachers we owe it to our students and to ourselves to keep developing and growing. This chapter looks at ways we might do that and how we might take the responsibility for our own growth into our own hands.

Understanding the why

I have deliberately used the word 'grow' in the title rather than CPD (continuing professional development), which can sound a little cold and remote and has the potential to remind us of the worst training days we have been on. We need to keep growing in life and in teaching. As teachers, we have three main reasons to do so:

1 Keeping up – Given all the changes that occur in education on a constant basis it is important that we keep up-to-date with new developments. These may be developments in the subject area, developments in technology, developments in teaching method, and new specifications. Each of these require that we grow and develop in order not to be left behind.

2 Confidence – Developing our skills and becoming good at something develops our confidence. We have already established the psychological importance of confidence (see chapter 17). One way to feel that you are up to the job is to actually be up to the job!

3 Nonsense radar – One of the best antidotes to being told what to do is to read up on better ways to do it and then get on with actually doing it! Growing and learning enables us to have a built in nonsense radar. There is a danger that as teachers we can become too busy to reflect on teaching methods; this means we can end up swallowing everything that we are told, despite some speakers' lack of experience in the classroom.

Don't leave it to the school

You probably don't need me to tell you that CPD provision is extremely variable across schools and colleges; there is a risk that this may even get worse as budgets become tighter. Too often the INSET day is a one size fits all, whole staff event. At its poorer end, it is essentially a long briefing in which information that could have been emailed is read slowly from a PowerPoint. At the better end, I have been to inspirational sessions that have had a direct impact on what I have done with classes – but that's perhaps three or four days, at best. Given that I have been teaching almost 20 years and have had 5 INSET days each year, that perhaps isn't saying much.

I feel terrible in saying this, but psychologically the best approach to whole staff training days is to expect little. That way you are likely to be pleasantly surprised; remember, even if you learn one useful tip, it has been worth it. Also do not assume that you will have lots of free time to do planning or tidying up; CPD sessions are directed time. If your headteacher wants to plan your day for you to the minute, that is his or her right. Don't go in expecting time and you will not resent losing it.

Either way, as a professional, your growth is not entirely the school or college's responsibility. So welcome good CPD when it comes your way in school, but don't expect all of it to be transformative! Start to take some responsibility for your own growth.

Leadership byte

If you are responsible for the organisation of CPD within your area, it is worth reflecting on the approach you wish to take. Just as you would differentiate in class for individual needs, it is unlikely that your staff require exactly the same input at exactly the same time.

Try to have discussions with your staff regarding their needs and allow alternative provision, such as attendance at teach-meets and enrolments on external accredited courses, to count. Do what you can to facilitate and reward staff who are taking an interest in their own development.

Taking control in school

There are a number of things that you can do in your school context to ensure that you keep growing:

1 First, honestly take stock of where you are. Look at the descriptors of good teaching and/or good subject leadership and measure yourself against them. Use observation feedback where appropriate, although be aware that at times observation can be a little bit of a game; peer observation from a trusted colleague may yield more realistic information.

2 Take the opportunity to watch others teach. The days of every teacher's classroom being a locked kingdom are very much over, but this does not need to be threatening. Try to watch other practitioners in your school or college teach, particularly those that you know or have heard are good teachers. Explain what you are hoping to see before you appear, and say thank you as you leave.

3   Share your own expertise: where you have developed a skill or an area of expertise, open up your classroom or seek to deliver a session to others. This is a great confidence boost, and as we know one of the ways that we learn most is through teaching others; that's why we keep our students explaining things to each other!

Taking control out of school

I recognise that this may sound like extra work and decidedly out of place in a book about reducing stress. However, putting some of our focus into our growth and development is short term pain for long term gain. Part of our development as teachers and part of not feeling so stressed about everything is to be on top of things and to develop our skills. There are a number of things we can do:

1   Read books – The suggestions for further reading listed at the end of this book show a number of the books that I have read in the last two or three years. Read books on teaching and learning; read books on leadership, psychology or spirituality that will aid your personal development. Read and absorb information. Reflect on and challenge what you read. You may only get one or two little gems from a book, but they could be important. Why not set up a staff library so that staff can share books?

2   Edu-Twitter – Join the education community on Twitter. There are lots of excellent teachers posting links to blogs and articles on Twitter. At present, I consider Twitter to be the primary source of information, news and articles about teaching and learning, policy changes and education news. If you want to draw personal and professional boundaries, there is no reason why you cannot have a second Twitter account purely for you as a teacher.

3   Writing – Writing is a great way of reflecting and clarifying your thoughts on an issue. Whether your writing is in the form of a personal journal or you are adventurous and want to try blogging, writing helps. If you do blog, you will be surprised at what connections can be developed.

4   Teachmeets – Teachmeets are a reaction I suspect to the tedium of some official staff development days. They are informal CPD

organised by teachers for teachers. There is usually food and short, fun presentations. Information on where and when teachmeets are occurring can be found on the main teachmeet website (http:// teachmeet.pbworks.com).

5 Further Study – One of the ways to ensure we keep growing is to undertake further study. This could be a leadership course, an MA or other accredited courses. Ask your school or college whether they are willing to part fund or give time. You don't know if you don't ask!

Above all try to develop specialisms and possibly sidelines, such as examination work or event organising. This will enable you to become the go to SEN expert, literacy expert, technology expert in your school; grow your expertise and your specialisms now and they will be of use to you either now or later.

 Questions for reflection

1 What has been the best CPD you have had? What did you learn? Why was it so good?

2 Where are you now in terms of your skills? What areas are you looking to develop? Honestly are you growing?

3 What specialisms are you developing or are going to develop? How might you use these now and in the future?

Bibliography

Cowley, S (2009) *Teaching Skills for Dummies*, Chichester: John Wiley & Sons.
Morrison McGill, Ross (2015) *Teacher Toolkit: Helping You Survive Your First 5 Years*, London: Bloomsbury.

Chapter 31

Teaching as a long game

Most of the things that really matter in life are not instantaneous. For instance parenthood is a long commitment. It will last at least 18 years, and that's being optimistic. Take relationships, as another example. Friendships, marriages, business partnerships all take time to nurture and develop and can probably be destroyed within minutes! Consider also talents and skills. To repeat a much used analogy, David Beckham required repeated practice to develop his skills at free kick taking. Ed Sheeran did not leave the womb playing the guitar well. It all takes time and energy.

Unfortunately one of the big obstacles we face in educating students is that society has increasingly gone the way of the instant. Coffee is instant, food is fast, and a world of information is available on hand held devices. It can be tempting to sacrifice the truly great for the here and now. This chapter looks at teaching as a 'long game' in which we need to focus on the future rather than the here and now.

Winning the battle but losing the war

The pressure of the instant also affects us as teachers; it is not just our students who feel it. We all know of colleagues who have completely changed a lesson to accommodate an observer; I have even heard tell of students being given exactly the same lesson that was practised before Ofsted came in! Likewise setting filler exercises so that we can catch up on admin or marking whilst the students are in the room may, on rare occasions, be a needs-must, but if the full spec isn't covered by the end of the year, it will come back to bite us in the form of after school sessions. The systems we work in often demand that we prioritise the short term at the expense of the long term. Whilst it can be tempting solely to teach to the exams, education and learning as opposed to the automatic remembering of facts to pass exams is important and significant. Like the other important things in life, it takes time. Education is a long game.

The long game in the classroom – with your students

Our students are digital natives. On an anecdotal level, it seems that they have shorter attention spans and ability to concentrate than students in 'the olden days'. Certainly perseverance can be a challenge. If a website does not yield the required information in a second, then we are away to the next site on the list. Likewise if an area of study is difficult, our students are turned away to the more immediate and easy. Instead:

1   We need to prepare our students for the long term challenge of education. Sharing the mindset ideas (chapter 29) is a good start, but anything that increases meta-cognition – thoughts about how we learn – is useful. A little questioning will show whether an answer from Google is merely being repeated or is actually understood.

2   As teachers we need to think scheme of work or year plans rather than lesson plans. It is important that we start with the end in mind – rather than deliver great lessons but end a month short of finishing the specification or deliver the Christmas topic in January. It sounds obvious, I know. Look at the range of activities – literacy, numeracy etc. – and assessment points over time rather than stressing about cramming everything into each lesson.

3   Recognise that learning is not linear. There will be ups and downs, times of progress and times of consolidation. Unfortunately this may not be appreciated by senior colleagues bearing spreadsheets, who ask why Aaliyah is still level 3b. Nevertheless, resist the temptation to bend the data to fit the desired curve. Teach consistently

well, focusing on the right things, and usually the data catches up. Don't be one of those teachers whose class data is excellent all year but is mysteriously under the average when external assessment occurs. Remember that time and truth are friends.

4   Deal with the roots: I am a lazy gardener, preferring quick rather than effective weeding. I tend to take the top off weeds on the grounds that if I can't see it, I won't worry about it. The weeds come back. It is the same with student issues: fail to deal with them and they return. Will you find out about how a dyslexic student works now or leave it? A seating plan devised in September may be better than trying to move students two months in as a response to trouble. Likewise a swift response to off task behaviour in week 1, or taking time to establish a relationship with a potentially challenging student, is better than trying to shut the stable door after the horse has bolted.

The long game of the classroom – career (noun) not career (verb)

One delightful and amusing feature of the English language is that career is both a noun and a verb. The difference between the two illustrates the long game approach rather nicely. Either we focus on our career or we career from one urgent, short term deadline to the next.

1   **Getting good at it.** Business leaders refer to the 10k principle. Put simply: if you want to be truly exceptional at something, then you have to put in about 10,000 hours doing that thing. Assuming we teach 20 hours a week for around 40 weeks of the year, my guess is that if the principle is correct, then no one is an expert teacher until they have done over 12 years! As mentioned in the previous chapter, take time to invest in your growth as a teacher, but go easy on yourself.

2   **Accept your limits.** As mentioned earlier, the long game of the academic year or the two year GCSE course is much more important than the individual lesson. Sometimes we have to be pragmatic and accept that each lesson we teach won't be outstanding. It's not physically possible. We are all aware of colleagues who were truly

talented yet perfectionistic, who worked themselves to the point of exhaustion. Perhaps some of their lessons were better than ours, but they had more time off sick, cried more tears in the staffroom and ultimately ended up leaving teaching. The importance of pacing ourselves cannot be over emphasised. Consistently good is better than one off perfection.

3   **Future proofing**. As happy as you are now in your current role, remember that there may come a time when you are ready to move on. Part of the long game of having a career is to develop the skills that you are likely to need at the next step. If you are unsure what those skills are, have a look at a job description for such a role when it is advertised, or arrange a conversation about what the role involves with someone in your institution who is in that post. As mentioned in the previous chapter, work on your specialisms and interests so that if you are in the position of choosing to or having to look for a new position, you become a strong contender.

?   Questions for reflection

1   What is your long term planning like compared to your lesson planning? Do you have clear long term aims?

2   What things do I need to do or put in place in September that will make my life a little easier the rest of the year?

3   Are there student issues that I am not properly dealing with that are likely to return and bite me later?

4   Am I thinking about possible next steps for my career? Am I focusing on things that will make me employable?

Chapter 32

Surviving the year

As soon as I know my timetable and have picked up the exam results, I can give some thought to the year. Just as a good driver does not look at the edge of the bonnet when she is driving but focuses as far ahead as she can see on the road, so too it is vital that we focus on our year as a whole – not just the week ahead. Teaching is a long game and it requires that we get organised. This chapter is about ensuring that we survive the year and, more than that, do so without any major balls falling to the floor.

One big document – the year planner

In order to ensure that I don't miss anything and am able to plan and schedule my work as much as possible, I use a year planner like that in Table 32.1. It is possible to do a similar thing with a calendar on a smartphone, but I like the visual nature of having one document that fits everything on. It is relatively easy to create and customise your own version based on the classes/courses you teach; you may or may not need all the columns that I use.

1   Notice that it has two columns for each course I teach – one for content, one for assessment and marking.

2   As a middle manager I have separated department, which includes things that I have initiated, and whole college.

3   As a senior examiner and writer, I have an external column in addition to the most important column – my life outside work.

Table 32.1 Year Planner

Date	Course 1 RS AS		Course 2 RS A2		Course 3 Phil A2		Dpt	Whole College	External	Other
7/9	Induction	F1	Virtue	F1	Plato text		Results Review for SLT		Remarks for Exam board	
14/9	Induction		Virtue	soc	Plato text	F1	Marketing info. Literacy Analysis			
21/9	Plato	S1	Virtue	S1	Plato text	S1	Induction Review Learner Voice			Dad Birthday 24/9
28/9	Plato/Aristotle	Exam Tech.	Soul/Life after death	Exam tech	Appearance and Reality	Exam Tech	Review Week	Parents Eve A2 30/9		
5/10	Aristotle		Soul/Life after death	F2	Appearance and Reality	F2	Marketing			
12/10	Biblical God	F2	Soul/Life after death		Political Rule				Ukedchat article due	Son Birthday 12/10
19/10	Biblical God	S2	Conscience	S2	Political Rule	S2	1–1's + review	INSET 23rd		
2/11	Teleological		Conscience	S2	Knowledge and Virtue		1–1's + review	Reports to Parents AS		Family Christening Sunday 8th
9/11	Teleological		Religious Experience	soc	Moral Phil/Utilitarianism	F3	S2 IVReview Week	Open Eve 2 10/11		
16/11	Evil	F3	Religious Experience	F3	Utilitarianism	soc		Parents Eve 18/11	SASCAL 19/11	
23/11	Cosmological	soc	Religious Experience	soc	Deontology	F3	Visiting speaker – Islamic community (Mon–Thurs)	Open Eve 25/11	New spec meeting 27/11 (TBC)	Parents Eve (daughter's sch.) 26/11

Setting up your planner

1   **Know your dates**. Exam boards publish their exam dates over a year in advance. Your college or school should have a calendar detailing open evenings, when each year group has its parents evening, when reports are to be written, mock exam weeks, year 6 residentials, school productions, any whole school assessment points that are fixed etc. Insert these into your year planner. There is nothing more frustrating to a manager than staff being oblivious to published dates and deadlines. Take some responsibility here.

2   **Know roughly what you will be teaching**. Look at your scheme of work for each class/topic or year group. Put in roughly where you will be each week. Things may change, but it will help you see roughly where you are in relation to where you need to be.

3   **Identify your assessments**. Put in your assessments. Where you have flexibility, put them on lighter weeks; try not to set every class a piece of work the same week. As you can see above, despite having fixed assessment deadlines, it is possible to spread the marking load by moving a course a week early. Put quicker, easier assessments, such as a Socrative quiz, for busy weeks.

4   **Know your pressure points**. Look at the detailed document you now have. This will show you your pressure points. Look again at what you can move, particularly if you are a middle manager. Make sure you don't take other things on during those weeks.

5   **Slot in the 'what else' accordingly**. You will have other things that need to be accomplished, such as performance management targets, event organisation and targeted support for students. Fit these accordingly where there is space.

Accept that you will lose a few hours setting this up, possibly at a weekend at the start of term, but it will be worth it. In addition to a printed version, it may also be worth having it on Google Docs or Dropbox so that it is on hand at all times, including when you are stopped in a corridor and asked for your availability on a certain date.

Sort out your classes

Once you have a sense of times and dates, the other important thing to set up are your classes. Your markbook will need class data, space for assessment marks, and a couple of seating plans. If you are an iPad user, the IDoceo App (see www.idoceo.net) is excellent. It allows all of the above and has a class schedule and name selector for random questioning. Get your school to buy a lead that connects the iPad to your projector and classes can get off to a crisp start.

You may also wish to set up Google Classroom for each of your students. This allows you to set and mark work electronically and works well particularly with older students. Sort out your physical classroom too. Give some thought to procedures (e.g. having a folder that contains spare sheets for those who have been away) and the layout of the room. Again it may take an hour or two, it may even be after school, but you will be glad you've done it once term starts.

One half term at a time – 6 by 6

In his book *Axiom* (2008), Bill Hybels reflects on the difficulties that individuals have when they are working on too many things at once. The strategy suggested, '6 by 6', involves a question – what six things do you need to achieve in the next 6 weeks? This translates well for teachers because most of our half terms are 6–7 weeks long and, if we're honest, six things is about the most we can keep in our heads at any one time.

Obviously the bread and butter of our job – planning lessons and teaching them – isn't there; we would do that anyway! But for those times when we are not in front of a class – what will our key priorities be? Below is an example of the list that we used in our department last spring. It is mainly things that we would have been doing anyway, but the key word is focus: it sharpens the mind and ensures that the important things (Covey Quadrant boxes I and II; see chapter 27) get done. This is especially important as there will inevitably be urgent distractions at times.

An example: RS and philosophy spring term 2 (February to Easter)

During this half term, our main aim was to make good use of the mock exam and other assessments as well as help students transition to more independent revision. Independent learning was also a performance management objective during that year

What?

PRIORITY 1: Mock Exam review – Go through the paper; 1–1s with students, particularly those who underperformed. Information given to HoD for mid-year review; photocopy exemplar scripts. Detailed data analysis by HoD.

PRIORITY 2: Use F5 Formative assessment – Differentiated and focusing on students at risk to develop essay technique or Stretch and challenge. Feedback need not be as detailed for all students.

PRIORITY 3: Use S5 Summative assessment – Carefully marked and detailed feedback given. This is the last timed essay that has the possibility of impact before exams (S6 may be too late!).

PRIORITY 4: Revision Launch – Lesson on revision skills and exam technique 2 months before exams (mid-March for AS, end of March for A2). Publish revision materials, make revision materials visible on VLE.

PRIORITY 5: INDEPENDENT LEARNING (the content) – Each class to have at least one Socrative or other similar test to check independent learning of past content. Teacher to take a snapshot of VLE use; who is working? Who is not?

PRIORITY 6: INDEPENDENT LEARNING (the skills) – 'File check Friday' event; students bring or show notes for teacher to check; prioritise those at risk first. Use this and S5 results to generate list for Learning Mentor support.

Table 32.2 6 by 6 Planning: An Example

Week (wb)	1. Mock	2. F5	3. S5	4. Revision	5. IL – content	6. IL – skills
23/2	Complete Marking + mid year review				AS SOC	
2/3	Mock review lesson and 1–1				A2 SOC	
9/3		F5 marking		AS Launch		AS File check
16/3		F5 1–1s where needed	AS S5 completed		AS VLE audit	
23/3			S5 mark Update at risk list	A2 Launch		A2 File check
30/3			A2 S5 + mark Update at risk list		A2 VLE	

? Questions for reflection

1 Do you find yourself constantly asking colleagues when events or deadlines are? Why is that? Would something similar to the Year Planner help?

2 What degree of flexibility do you have with regard to assessments and other activities? What can you do to avoid everything coming at once?

3 How do you ensure that those key Covey Quadrant box II things happen even when you are busy?

Bibliography

Hybels, B (2008) *Axiom – Powerful Leadership Proverbs*, Zondervan: Michigan.

Chapter 33

Surviving the week

Having a big picture that shows all the things you should be doing week by week is one thing, but actually organising the week is another. It is no good us saying that we are overwhelmed by the things we have got to do if, when we are asked how we are going to do things, we reply, 'I'll do it at some point.' This chapter looks at weekly organisation and focuses on how you can get most (but probably not all) of your jobs done each week.

The weekly planner

Table 33.1 shows my main tool for organising my week: my weekly planner. Again the table is easy to produce and you may be able to customise it. As with the year planner, I will link to Google drive or Dropbox to ensure it is available to me more readily.

A few things are worth pointing out about setting up such a table:

1   You may or may not be a morning person. Feel free to use different columns if you are an owl not a lark!

2   Look for your pressure points, remembering that it is important to manage your energy rather than your time. A day could start at 5.30 a.m. or could go on until 11 p.m., but I know that is not desirable all 5 days. Also, I know that I will not get much done on a Thursday because I teach all day. Accept that and don't worry. Roughly count the hours that you are planning to work,

Table 33.1 Weekly Planner

Day	Very early 5:30–7:00 a.m.	Before work 7:30–8:45 a.m.	8:45–10:15 a.m.	10:30–12:00 p.m.	Lunch	12:45–2:15 p.m.	2:30–4:00 p.m.	After work 4:00–6:00 p.m.	Evening 7:00–9:00 p.m.
Mon			RS A2 col A	RS AS col B	Lunch	RS A2 col C			
Tues			DPT MEETING 9–10 a.m.	RS AS col E	Lunch	Phil A2 col F	RS A2 col A		
Wed			RS AS col B	RS A2 col C	Lunch		Revision/catch up slot		
Thu			RS AS col E	Phil A2 col F	Lunch	RS A2 col A	RS AS col B		
Fri			RS A2 col C		Lunch	RS AS col E	Phil A2 col F		1
Sat			2			3		4	
Sun			5			6		7	
					Home +			Weekend	
1. Urgent/Important		2. Important/Not urgent							
Planning Student Issues									
3. Urgent/Not important		4. Not urgent/Not important							

remembering that going over 55 adds nothing. (see chapter 14 on boundaries).

3   Notice that planning and student issues are a standing order in Covey Quadrant box I. Get these right and you are doing the job you have been employed to do.

4   Look for the gaps where you could really crack on with planning and admin. This year Monday afternoon gives me 3 hours if I stay past 5 p.m. Wednesday afternoon is also good on weeks when there is no revision or catch up. Look to block time; if you have a free last thing or first thing, consider that as a day when you come in early or stay late.

5   Think about rest. When will you be able to have your midweek evening off? This year it seems to be Wednesday, although if there is an evening event on Wednesday, it can move. The point is that one evening each week, you should leave on time, taking no work with you. Make sure you are getting 8 hours sleep a night.

6   Make the most of your weekend. Often we hear colleagues say that they worked all weekend. That's criminal! The weekend actually comes in seven parts; aim to work a maximum of one part – maybe two if you are extremely busy.

Patterns of working

There are various patterns of working. Which one works for you will be a combination of your body clock and your situation in life. It is worth experimenting to find what works best. The main options are a combination of the ideas below:

1   **Stay in school**. It is surprising how much you can get done in school if you are able to work longer days. By being on site a hour before the students and by staying until 5:30 p.m. most days, I have been able to get quite a lot done and reduce the work I take home significantly.

2   **Working at home**. Of course it may be that you work better at home, surrounded by familiar things and comfort. Depending on family responsibilities, this may involve early mornings, early

evenings or late nights once children are in bed. Again it is about finding what works.

3   **Biting the bullet – holidays or weekends**. One way of making the working week less stressful is to bite the bullet and use weekends and holidays to get ahead. It may be worth accepting a 6 day week if the days are genuine 8 hour days or accepting 2–3 weeks holiday lost in order to make the working weeks more humane.

Whatever pattern you adopt, do so consciously and plan. Don't fall into habitual, unplanned patterns of working or be vague. You will be constantly under pressure and will feel guilty every moment you aren't working.

Make a date with yourself

This planner is something I complete at the end of each week. It is in effect my clocking off ritual at around 5:00 p.m. each Friday. I look ahead to the next week: what will need to be done? When will I take time off? I feed in anything from my year planner that is coming up in the next week or so. Then I try to work out when each of the things on the list will get done.

Yes, but how? Practically speaking

The worked example in Table 33.2 shows a particularly busy recent week:

1   Given that there is an open evening on Tuesday, Wednesday has to be the evening off, and I will try to leave as close to 4 p.m. as possible.

2   I have to accept that little admin will get done on Thursday – or if it does, it needs to be things that require little energy.

3   There will need to be two early starts – I mark better and quicker in a morning, so mock marking is done there when possible.

4   It is likely that some work will spill into the weekend – I will aim to do things that I find vaguely enjoyable rather than tedious.

Table 33.2 Example of a Weekly Planner

Day	Very early 5:30–7:00 a.m.	Before work 7:30–8:45 a.m.	8:45–10:15 a.m.	10:30–12:00 p.m.	Lunch	12:45–2:15 p.m.	2:30–4:00 p.m.	After work 4:00–6:00 p.m.	Evening 7:00–9:00 p.m.
Mon	Mocks (5 scripts)	Planning	RS A2 col A	RS AS col B	Lunch	RS A2 col C	Mocks (5 scripts)	Mocks (5 scripts) Teachmeet/conference (liaise with marketing	
Tues		Mocks (5 scripts)	DPT MEETING 9–10 a.m.	RS AS col E	Lunch	Phil A2col F	RS A2 col A	OPEN EVENING	OPEN EVENING 8 p.m.
Wed		Mocks (5 scripts)	RS AS col B	RS A2 col C	Lunch	Planning for Th/Fr	Revision/ catch up slot	NIGHT OFF	NIGHT OFF
Thurs		Mocks (5 scripts)	RS AS col E	Phil A2 col F	Lunch	RS A2 col A	RS AS col B	Mid-year review and tracking	
Fri	Mocks (5 scripts)	Mocks (5 scripts)	RS A2 col C	Planning Mon/Tues	Lunch	RS AS col E	Phil A2 col F	Check weekly planner – leave ASAP	1

			3 Mindset Programme	4
Sat				
Sun		5	6	7
		Home +		Weekend

1. Urgent/Important	2. Important/Not urgent
Planning Student Issues Mock Marking (40 scripts by Friday) Mid-Year review and tracker Promote Teachmeet and Conference	Philosophy A2 SoW Revision documents Go through exam scripts (A2 students) Review 'mindset programme'
3. Ugent/Not important	4. Not urgent/Not important
VLE audit Phil A2 Performance Management Update	Tickets for Conference

Part of being a teacher is recognising that you will never finish every-thing, but that's okay – no one can. Hopefully some of the thoughts above will help us to reflect on our priorities and get the important things done!

? **Questions for reflection**

1 Do you find lists of things to do overwhelming? Do you some-times procrastinate when it comes to the job you least like?

2 Would a weekly planner or something like it help you to be more organised?

Chapter 34

Surviving the day

Teaching in an imaginary parallel universe where you are left alone by managers, not shamed by league tables or hectored by dim politicians and journalists is a very simple job. It really is 'mark, plan, teach, repeat' (Morrison McGill 2015, p. 5). Sometimes, in a full day's teaching, the above can occur, even in our flawed universe. On other days we have admin to contend with. This chapter deals with the mechanics of surviving the day as a teacher.

Things you only know if you teach a full day

Some days as teachers we have the joy of the full day: 5–6 hours of back to back lessons. If you are really lucky, you may have two each week. If you have a different role, in which you don't teach full time or you are now promoted so that much of your time is outside the classroom, it is worth reminding yourself of those things that you only know if you teach a full day:

1   **Your bladder.** At some point during the afternoon, you will become aware that you have not been to the toilet all day. You should have gone at break, but you were helping a student with work/dealing with an incident. You realise that it is still 30 minutes to the end of the lesson. This is the only half hour in the day that passes slowly.

2   **The best laid plans.** One of your lessons will almost certainly go wrong. You got in well before 8 a.m. and photocopied, put things

in neat piles, and saved changes to your presentations. Yet now it is 3:30 p.m., the last lesson of the day. You can't find the worksheet you need to save your life and the words coming out of your mouth are not really in full sentences. This is when a senior manager walks in.

3 **Too much information**. You will have an enormous number of interactions with students handing you work, telling you why they cannot hand in work, that they have a medical appointment, that mum is ill, passing messages about other students. Although you will be nowhere near a computer or notebook and doing something unrelated, they will expect you to remember what they said/did and be offended if you don't. After all, they only told you one thing – it is not their fault that so did the 100 other students you saw that day. When the day finishes you will slump in front of a computer and try to remember the things you need to pass on. You will alert other staff, log information, reply to emails. You will remember the one you forgot just as you are going to sleep that night.

4 **Voice**. Your voice will wear during the day. You will try to be more organised next week and carry lots of water to drink. But see point 1 – the decision about whether to look after your bladder or your voice is one of teaching's most profound conundrums.

5 **Email**. You will also arrive back in your office or staffroom to a flurry of emails. Some will by then have follow up emails expressing annoyance at the fact that you haven't replied. You have tried the strategy of keeping them open whilst you teach in previous years, but have learned that multitasking and teaching well do not go together.

6 **The things to do list**. You accept that the admin list will grow during the day, and the marking will increase. There will be other days where you will make progress on the list, but it might not be today. That's okay; we are serious about teaching and learning being the main thing, after all – aren't we?

7 When someone suggests you attend a meeting after work or come to a 'working lunch' on one of your full teaching days, you contemplate violence against that person.

You realise that you do genuinely love teaching; when it is going well, it is a great job even if it is tiring.

Surviving the full teaching day

Teaching a full day needs meticulous preparation. It begins the night before as you leave the building, when you check that the lessons are all at least prepared in outline and things that need copying have been copied. On the teaching day the following tips apply:

1   **Get in early.** It is miserable just getting to your first lesson/registration on time. You spend the day chasing yourself and never seem to recover.

2   **'Walk through your day'** in your head and if you are teaching in different rooms, leave relevant stuff in those rooms. Sort each lesson's resources into piles and check that tech (in particular clickers and iPad connectors) are where they should be.

3   **Slow yourself down.** Focus on one lesson at a time and walk a little slower. Try to be fully present in the moment.

4   **Notes.** Keep a notepad or Post-It® notes handy and write down things that you are told during the day that you need to do or remember.

5   **At the end of the day** – which is a little like coming off stage – have a brief downtime with a cup of tea and grab a chat with a colleague. When the adrenalin has stopped a few minutes later – go back to your Post-It® notes and log things. Check your emails!

Planning and marking

Planning

Planning good lessons takes time. Planning the perfect lesson takes even longer and then doesn't materialise because we are too weary to execute the plan properly! It is hard when you are new to teaching, but try not to overplan. Have a map of where the lesson is going but be prepared to be flexible. Consider the following:

1   Have a good electronic filing system and save everything. Even resources that don't work can be mended and modified. Be an electronic hoarder.

2   It's good to share. Don't be proud; if you are in a team, share planning and swap resources. Have a departmental Dropbox account,
join TES resources and connect with others on UKEdchat. Find
subject specific or key stage specific sites that allow sharing.

3   Have go to strategies for AfL. Students often don't know what we
think they should know. Have some strategies with which you can
take the temperature of the learning, as it were, at key points. It
may be a quiz on Socrative or Kahoot; it may be with mini-white-
boards, Post-It® notes, red/green cards or by random Q & A. Have
two or three that you are comfortable with and use them regularly.

4   Avoid 'last lesson on earth' syndrome. In other words, resist the
tendency to throw absolutely everything in. Remember that differentiation, numeracy, equality and diversity, SEAL etc. are to be
covered as appropriate over time. If your seating is right, that's a
start with differentiation, in any case.

Marking

Marking is an essential part of teaching, but it threatens to become a
monster; it has been highlighted as the main workload issue. Teachers can spend every waking moment marking if they are not careful. I
once caught a teacher marking books whilst we waited at a wedding.
What, if anything, can we do to lighten the load?

1   Does everything need marking? Clearly the answer is no. It links
back to having a clear purpose for work that we set. Is it a summative assessment – in which case, it may just need a mark – or a
formative assessment, where we are hoping to develop skills? This
may need more of a comment.

2   Does everything need to be marked by me? Peer marking can be
effective if students understand the criteria used. For exam groups
it can be an excellent exercise to try to apply a markscheme and
think like an examiner.

3   Do I need to mark it out of hours? Marking in class using verbal feedback can be highly effective – sometimes more so than
providing purely written feedback. If the class is working on

a task, could you be circulating and marking? Where students are asked to improve work, could they do this in class and show you rather than hand it in again? Likewise setting self-marking quizzes via Socrative or Kahoot can give instant feedback to students.

4 Do I physically need to mark this and write long feedback? Even if we end up having to mark out of class, there are some shortcuts: pre-printed stickers or a comment bank may be options given that students may make similar errors. One of my favourite current tools when work is submitted in Google Apps or Google Classroom is the microphone on my iPad. It types whatever you speak onto the work – but do check it before sending as it can mishear!

We will probably never totally beat the marking load, but there are some additional time savers in the suggested reading list at the end of this book. In addition, @teachertoolkit's 5 minute lesson plan and 5 minute marking plan come highly recommended (see http://www.teachertoolkit.me).

Administration

On some of your days you find that you have a free lesson, some PPA time or an hour before you go home. It can be a shock to the system. The temptation to waste it, as it is only an hour or so, is strong: 15 minutes drinking tea and catching up on Facebook, 15 minutes looking at the list and wondering where to start and then there seems little point starting anything. Much has already been said in previous chapters about having a list of priorities and planning when things will be done. Hence, these are merely additional tips:

1 Do the job you are dreading first. It could be marking or phoning that difficult parent; psychologically it feels better when it is done.

2 If there is something on your list that can be done in 5–10 minutes, do it there and then.

3 If you have a large list and feel overwhelmed, slow down, pick one of the items off the list and start it.

> **?** **Questions for reflection**
>
> 1 How can you save planning time? Can you plan collabora-
>   tively or use online communities? Are you able to let go of
>   perfectionism and plan lessons that are good enough?
>
> 2 What strategies can you use to speed up marking? Can you
>   cut the quantity and keep the quality?
>
> 3 Do you procrastinate when you have a free period? What can
>   you do to avoid this?

Bibliography

Cowley, S (2009) *Teaching Skills for Dummies*, Chichester: John Wiley & Sons.
Morrison McGill, R (2015) *Teacher Toolkit: Helping You Survive Your First 5 Years*, London: Bloomsbury.
Smith, J (2010) *The Lazy Teacher's Handbook*, Camarthen: Crown House.

Part 5

The others

Chapter 35

Meet the team – your students

Having survived my NQT year, I naïvely assumed that the job in the classroom would get easier. In my second year I met 10 set 4. They were a bigger group than one would have liked given the range of educational needs and behavioural issues. Their science teacher did no practical work with them, their Maths and English teachers insisted on a Teaching Assistant (TA). They were broken up for option subjects. This was RE – important enough to be compulsory yet not important enough to get a TA; they were doing a GCSE short course against their will, and their only lesson was last thing in the afternoon. It was a very long year.

Perhaps one of the more irritating claims that is made, usually by those who are no longer in the classroom, is that if you plan interesting lessons then attendance and behaviour are automatically sorted. Whilst there is some truth in the fact that poor planning can increase misbehaviour, we have to be careful about accepting the responsibility and blame for things that are outside our control. Our students come to us with a range of difficulties and situations that are going on in their lives; our lessons may rank quite low in their list of concerns. This chapter deals with the behaviour and underlying emotions in the classroom and how we can be more aware of this when managing our classes.

You are the adult

Many of us have had a laugh at the Internet meme that describes how in some situations we can still look around for an adult – someone more competent than we feel – to take charge. In the classroom you are the adult in the room; although sometimes we can be fun, we can be slightly anarchic; we are ultimately responsible for the class. We are 'en loco parentis'.

Sometimes, whether we like it or not, we have to address the parent things before we can address the teacher things; remember Maslow's hierarchy of needs (introduced in chapter 6). If your students do not feel comfortable and safe within your room or are anxious over your lesson or something else, their brains may not be switched on to learning and self-actualisation; striking the right balance between safety and challenge in our manner and in the activities is quite an art.

Modern education has become clinical and dehumanising. It is important that we connect with our students and give them the impression that we care about them and like them – most of the time, we genuinely do! They are not a series of reds and greens on a tracking sheet. Even if you don't think that student mental health and wellbeing is your job – I think you're wrong – address it anyway because it improves relationships and learning.

Managing the emotions

As the adult in the room, you are the manager of the emotions in the room; whether they originate with you or not, you are responsible for dealing with them. You are able to set the climate of the room with your own emotions and manage the weather by how you respond to the behaviour and actions of others. What has been said previously about emotional intelligence applies here:

1   **Remember that self-esteem is a very powerful thing**. We all want to be respected. That includes your students; respect does cut both ways. One way of remembering this is to RIP and PIP (Reprimand in Private and Praise in Public). Do all you can to diffuse situations rather than blow them up. One of the big mistakes I made in my early career was to blow situations up by reacting angrily and publicly to misbehaviour. This leaves the student with nowhere to go but to react in kind in order to save face.

2   **Tune in, redirect, thank you**. One excellent way of dealing with this is shown in Bill Rogers' book *Managing Teacher Stress* (1992): he models the technique of tuning in, redirecting and saying thank

you. Rogers gives the example of a student eating crisps in class and initially refusing to put them away as they are 'only crisps'. Rather than shouting or making a big thing of this 'defiance', the teacher responds, 'I know they are (tune in), but I want you to put them in your bag or on my desk (redirection). Thanks, Gavin' (Rogers 1992, p. 37).

3   **Individuals not the class.** The use of names shown above is important – not just because it focuses your remarks on the individual but also because it shows that you are aware of them as an individual. On this theme, remember that most of the class will generally be compliant and on your side. Yelling 'all of you quieten down' when five people are speaking, or giving a whole class detention, is a great way to alienate students. Remember how you feel when the headteacher spends 10 minutes in a staff meeting berating everyone because two or three people (and you know who they are) arrive late to their classes. Don't be so focused on the few who are challenging that you forget to manage the emotions of the compliant majority.

4   **Manage your own emotions**. It is easy to become angry or despondent in class. Remember that behaviour is not personal and is not a threat to you even if it seems that way. Remember that one of your classroom strategies not working is not equivalent to you being a failure as a person. This is an example of your inner chimp catastrophising or, as Goleman (1995) suggests, 'sloppy emotional thinking'. Remember that you are not just a teacher (see chapter 13).

Finally, in terms of emotions, recognise when 'not to poke the bear' and to know when you are beaten; if something is not working in class, pause and present an alternative as though you had planned it all along. There are some days when, for a variety of reasons, plan A will not work.

Practically speaking

In terms of managing behaviour in the classroom, prevention is better than cure.

Prevention

1   Give thought to the layout of your room and the seating plan for your class/classes. For most of your classes, a seating plan is one of your most important strategies for managing the group. If you are using IDoceo, you can load pre-prepared seating plans and have them projected onto the board as the students arrive.

2   A starter activity on the desk as students arrive, with a timer counting down on the board, is a good strategy for getting things moving, particularly with difficult groups. Having a competitive twist to the activity may also help engagement, particularly of the boys in the group (e.g. how many answers can you find in five minutes)?

3   Finally, in terms of prevention, use the room. Don't be afraid to move around towards students who may be off task so that you can have a private word. It is your room, but respect personal space; getting too close will be perceived as aggressive.

Cure

1   Use your eyes. Make sure that as you are speaking your eyes are moving around the room, perhaps resting upon those who are fidgeting. A well placed glance or stare can often be better than using your voice.

2   Use choice. When you have to discipline a student, make sure that a choice is offered. 'Either you put the phone away or I will have to refer this to the head of year; it's up to you, Yasmin. Thank you.'

3   Use the policy. Be clear on your school policy with regard to expectations and sanctions and follow it consistently; this helps the students know where they are and is also a back up to you if someone tries to argue that you have not dealt with the situation appropriately.

4   Use the team. Behaviour management is tricky and we can all have bad days; it's not just new teachers. Know when to call a friend, either to ask how they deal with a situation or whether they mind you watching them teach the same class. Likewise use senior staff if there is serious misbehaviour.

Finally, if there is a difference between what you say and what you do, guess which one the students will follow and take as their cue. Your actions do speak louder than words. Make sure that you follow through on things that you say you are going to do. This applies to giving rewards as well.

? **Questions for reflection**

1 What affects your moods in the classroom? Do you sometimes pass this on to the students?

2 Which of the strategies for managing behaviour do you already use? Which do you think could work for you in your setting?

Bibliography

Cowley, S (2009) *Teaching Skills for Dummies*, Chichester: John Wiley & Sons.

Goleman, Daniel (1995) *Emotional Intelligence – Why It Can Matter More Than IQ*, New York: Bloomsbury.

Peters, Steve (2011) *The Chimp Paradox*, London: Vermilion.

Rogers, William (1992) *Managing Teacher Stress*, London: Prentice Hall.

Chapter 36

Meet the crew – a beginner's guide to the staffroom

When you first arrive in a staffroom, it can be a daunting place. Some teachers can be territorial over mugs and chairs; recently a new staff member at college asked me how the coat pegs worked and whether people had designated pegs. Thankfully we are not that kind of staffroom!

Whilst there are not quite the eccentric characters that seemed to dwell in the staffrooms of my early years, there are strong characters nonetheless and some of them need careful handling. Get it right, and some of these people will be life savers for you and you for them. This chapter deals with relationships in the staffroom and how we can use them to survive and flourish.

Four to avoid or manage

We all know the people in the staffroom or any other workplace that we need to avoid. They may be very nice people, but they are just no good for us. They do not make us feel better, they do not make us work better – we just feel worse when we spend time with them.

> **Priya Perfect**: Priya bounces in Tigger like each morning. She is an exceptional teacher, she says so herself! Whenever you share a success, she goes one better. Got a difficult class? She has a strategy. Concerned about the reporting deadline? She finished last week. The net result is that you leave the conversation

feeling worse. Whether Priya really is that good or whether it is a bluff based on her insecurity only time will tell. Avoid people who cause you to feel inferior even if it is inadvertently.

Stressed Out Sue: Sue is permanently anxious. Despite emails, announcements and notices on walls, she expresses astonishment that the deadline is this week. She seeks out sympathetic members of the staff to talk at length about her stress and workload. When she is less emotional, you may suggest strategies to help, but she seems to throw off constructive ideas. Sue is a martyr, and you just don't understand – no one does!

Weary Will: Will is the Eeyore of the staffroom. His glass isn't even half empty. In fact, it broke a long time ago and they expect him to clear it up. Will has no joy in teaching and is counting down every one of the 31 years to his retirement. As you serve up an optimistic remark in his general direction, pessimism is fired back at you faster than a Federer return. Although some of his views may have a grain of truth, being around Will is draining.

Poisonous Pete: Pete brings a different type of negativity to the staffroom. He is critical of school initiatives, critical of younger staff and their different methods, critical of those promoted ahead of him. Pete is a gossip and spreads things he has heard or heard that someone has heard without any care as to their truth or falsity. Regardless of his abilities in the classroom, Pete destabilises the staffroom.

Three people you need on your team

Having skilfully dodged the above and many more, there are three people that you need on your team. Sometimes these roles may be played by just one person, at other times they may be shared. These people may or may not be part of your actual team, but for the sake of sanity, you need to find them and develop your professional relationships:

1   **The Critical Friend**: Our job, like many jobs, demands high performance, and it is always possible to improve. The critical friend is able to offer suggestions and feedback on how you are doing. They are not afraid to tell you gently if you have messed up! Notice,

however, that they are a critical friend. There are plenty of crit-ics in teaching – media, Ofsted, consultants, uninformed people at the pub. Everyone is a critic. But the best critic is the one who in offering a 'critique' – things both good and bad – is on our side, genuinely cares for our welfare and wants to see us flourish to the best of our ability. They accept your imperfections and encourage you to rise above where you currently are.

2   **The Confidante**: We are not perfect, and we will make mistakes. Yet because of the culture of monitoring and accountability, we may be tempted to cover up our mistakes and put on our happy 'I'm fine' face. The reality is that year 10 were throwing chairs in your lesson, you're two weeks behind on marking and the kids at home have the flu. There needs to be someone for each of us that we can just be ourselves with and be vulnerable and honest about where we are at. This is an impossible job and we will all fall short at times. To have someone who will listen and not judge or think less of us is a source of powerful moral support.

3   **The Cheerleader**: It was Mark Twain who once said that he could live for two months on the strength of a good compliment. Sadly praise may be in short supply in many workplaces. Each of us needs a cheerleader for those Monday mornings when we wonder why we are doing this and whether we will be appreciated at all. I have joked that if anyone were ever mad enough to put me in charge I would issue an iPod to each member of staff and, in addi-tion to their favourite upbeat tracks, there would be a 30 second track of applause that they could listen to on the walk to the class-room. I don't have any hard evidence, but I'm convinced that we would all teach better on the strength of it. Find at least one person in the staffroom who thinks you are fantastic and make sure you spend time with them.

Your role in the staffroom

Of course being part of a staff isn't just something that happens to us; we have a part to play ourselves. We can take on the roles above for others; it is particularly important that we are cheerleaders for oth-ers in our school or college. We do not know people's situations, and often a kind word can make the difference between having a good or bad day.

Simple acts of kindness go a long way in a staffroom. If you are free the lesson before break, could you make the coffee for others every now and then? If it is your birthday or it's just a dull Monday in January, why not bring in cake? This also extends to the support team in your school, who can sometimes wrongly perceive themselves as second class citizens to the teaching staff. Be friendly to office staff and the site team; not only is it the right thing to do, but they have far more influence than you think.

? **Questions for reflection**

1 Of course we wouldn't ever be like the four people to avoid, would we? Honestly what tendencies might you have? How can you behave better?

2 Are there some people in the staffroom that it would be better if you spent less time with? Which relationships could you develop instead?

3 How is your support network? Are there people at work or at home who can play the roles of critical friend, confidante and cheerleader?

Chapter 37

Meet the bosses – how to manage upwards

> Weekly planning . . . with learning objectives and success criteria for every area to head of year, due in Saturday 5 p.m. Feedback given on Sunday evening with suggestions for 'even better if.' This takes all day on a Saturday – so I have no weekend . . . I find it demoralizing and soul destroying that my class is outstanding and yet this gives the impression of lack of trust.
>
> (Classroom teacher quoted in DFE 2013, p. 21)

Researching for this book confirmed that there are some awful examples of leadership and management out there. This chapter looks at some of the worst things that managers do, as well as whether broadly speaking there are types of managers and what we can do to survive them.

The seven deadly leadership sins

Just as everyone remembers a good teacher, so too everyone remembers a bad leader. I have talked to many teachers and school staff at work, after church, over coffee at exam board meetings, over a beer with friends, and online whilst researching; between us, we have worked under hundreds if not thousands of leaders. Hence might I suggest that these are the seven leadership deadly sins:

1 Not knowing staff names.
2 Walking past people and blanking them.
3 Not practising what they preach.

4 Being inconsistent – what mood are they in today?

5 Inflexibility to new ideas or argument.

6 Lack of integrity or authenticity – playing politics.

7 Not appearing to care.

The last item on the list is particularly important. People have lives outside of work, and an occasional 'How are you?' and pausing to genuinely listen to the answer goes an awfully long way. One person I spoke to fondly recalled the headteacher of the large secondary school where he worked appearing on his doorstep one Saturday morning with a bunch of flowers the day after his mother had died.

Leadership styles and how to survive them

There are a number of different ways to categorise leadership and management styles. Daniel Goleman (2000) identifies six styles: the coercive, the authoritative, the democratic, the pacesetter, the affiliative and the coaching. Here briefly are three of the more difficult types to manage and how we may survive them:

1 **The Coercive Bully**. There are too many of these around currently, largely as a result of the huge pressure that schools are under. Unlike the authoritative leaders, who take time to explain the 'why' to their teams, the coercive leader merely issues directions; the effect, perhaps inadvertent, is to bully others. Remember, bullies are often being bullied themselves – possibly by Ofsted and government! Whilst doing your best to comply with all requests, it is also important to try to respectfully take a stand when a line is crossed. Try to do so with the support of colleagues. 'A group of middle managers feel . . .' carries more weight than 'I think . . .' Where staff are downtrodden, resistance is limited and you suspect you may be near the top of the hit list, keep a record of incidents, including exact words, times and dates. Join a union. Sorry to be negative!

2 **The Pacesetter**. The Pacesetter is a workaholic who seeks to lead by his or her own relentless example. They have so much drive that unfortunately the car is often far down the road without the passengers. They can be committed to their own method of doing things

and, unlike coaching leaders, are unable to recognise that there may be alternative ways of getting things done. Communication can become a difficulty. Make sure that you communicate upwards clearly and when you are unable to meet a deadline, explain why and state when it will be done. If you have found an alternative way of doing something, back up your case with evidence and offer it as a suggestion even if you are sure you are right!

3   **The Affiliative Leader.** These leaders find it difficult to come to decisions or, worse, make decisions and then reverse them. They don't want to upset anyone. This can be worse than the democratic leader, who will consult before making a decision; here decisions may be made slowly or even reversed if they are perceived to be unpopular. Offer them suggestions, and show them your reasoning on issues they are considering. Before acting on anything they have said, it may be worth checking in with them that this is still what they want: 'I think you said that but can I just clarify . . .'

Generally speaking

Of course leadership is challenging and your superiors may well be burdened with strategic problems that you know little about. Remember they have a greater level of responsibility in terms of the whole thing going wrong. It is easy for us to be overly critical. As a general consideration, be a good follower as much as you can:

1   Support decisions taken above you. Don't rubbish school policy in front of students; comply with directives. SIP and DIP (support in public and disagree in private) as you would with junior colleagues if you were a head of department.

2   Where you do disagree with a senior colleague, be courteous and use reasoned argument to explain your case. Be humble; it is a suggestion and you may be wrong. Most bosses are happy to have such dialogue, and it shows that you are thinking and care about what happens.

3   Take the weight where you can. Find out what issues your manager is working on and where you can offer solutions to these problems. This is a great way of showing that you are a proactive team player: 'I know that we haven't made a decision on which

exam board to use yet but I have done a little research and . . .' 'I wonder if one way of sorting the two year 6 classes is . . .'

Am I ready to lead?

> I firmly believe that you should master your classroom practice before you take on any additional roles within school.
>
> (Morrison McGill 2015, p. 173)

At some point, you may wonder whether to put yourself forward for a leadership position. Ross McGill is right to say that first of all you should be a good teacher; otherwise, you will lack integrity trying to lead others. Similarly it is important not to step forward for wrong reasons, such as ego or money.

It is also worth bearing in mind your teacher SHAPE – (School, Heart, Abilities, Personality and Experience – see chapter 11). This will prevent you from going for the wrong position. For example, although on paper I might seem a reasonable candidate for a Head of Year or Pastoral Assistant Head role, I know that it is not for me and I wouldn't do as good a job as I could in other areas.

One final thought on whether you are ready is that you may never feel ready, but that is irrelevant. Many people in leadership, even once successful, attest to the phenomenon of imposter syndrome – the feeling that sooner or later everyone is going to realise what a fraud they are! If you don't put yourself forward, then who else could get the job? Perhaps, like Plato's philosopher ruler, we should seek to lead, as the alternative is to be led by someone less talented!

? Questions for reflection

1. What things do you find difficult in your head of department or SLT? What type of leader might that person be? How could that leader be managed?

2. Are you a good follower? Are there issues that you could help your senior staff with? How can you be proactive?

3. Are you considering a promoted post? What sort of posts might suit your SHAPE? Look at some job descriptions for these posts.

Bibliography

DFE (2013) *Teacher workload diary survey 2013.* TNS BMRB. Available from https://www.gov.uk/government/uploads/system/uploads/attachment_data/file/285941/DFE-RR316.pdf (Accessed 30th December 2015).

Goleman, D (2000) Leadership That Gets Results. *Harvard Business Review*, March–April. Available from https://hbr.org/2000/03/leadership-that-gets-results (Accessed 18th February 2016).

Morrison McGill, R (2015) *Teacher Toolkit: Helping You Survive Your First 5 Years*, London: Bloomsbury.

Chapter 38

Meet the experts – handling the critics with care

I remember hearing an old recording of the late comedian Blaster Bates, who said that 'expert' was really two words: 'ex' – a 'has been' and 'spurt' – a 'drip under pressure'. Unfortunately some of our contact with experts is no laughing matter. The talented young secondary teacher who relayed the following anecdote to me is no longer in teaching:

> I thought the lesson went fairly well. The consultant gave me his feedback and told me he was giving a grade 3 – requires improvement. I was gutted as I knew that the report would go to SLT. Worse still, as he left the room he said, 'It perhaps was a grade 2 but I don't want you to get complacent.'

Experts seemed to multiply a few years ago, and they come in various forms: the consultant, the training provider, the inspector conducting a mock-sted. Given that we know that around half those leaving teaching each year (and that includes heads and deputies) remain in education, it is tempting to wonder how many float on the edges, earning quite lucrative daily rates as 'experts'.

Yet we also face another type of expert – less dangerous but equally annoying. We have the amateur expert at the school gate or over the garden fence. All of them by virtue of having once been to school have an opinion on how we do our job. In this category also we find the journalist whose opinion pieces in papers and online are treated as gospel by those who know no better. This chapter examines how we can cope with the expert, particularly the first kind.

Experts behaving badly

Anecdotes of poor experts such as the one at the start of the chapter are not unusual. We might add to that those experts who are taking money for old rope and transporting the same dull tedious PowerPoint to venue after venue. I am suspicious of anyone getting us into groups to brainstorm ideas. Having delivered some sessions myself, it is a great way to fill time, particularly if you are not entirely sure of the answers yourself. Likewise, for consultants, the strategy of an initial visit where comments are mainly negative followed by a return visit where, after watching essentially the same thing, mainly positive feedback is provided, seems to be more common than it should be. The consultant then duly takes credit for the improvement.

Who to listen to: two types of expert

It is difficult to spot the difference between good and bad experts initially. So it's important to approach each expert with an open mind and to be teachable. There are some truly great people who inspire, challenge and provide us with great strategies and tips for the classroom, and there are the others. One way of thinking about the difference is to come back to motive and, to borrow from the words of Jesus, consider the difference between the shepherd and the hireling; the shepherd is an expert who cares for the sheep, the hireling cares about being paid. The good expert is likely to have some of the following traits:

1   **They are close to their subject.** They have very recent experience of success in the area that they are talking about. It is impossible to give classroom teachers good advice if you have not lifted a board pen in anger for 10 years. The world has moved on a little. True experts have authenticity and authority in their area of expertise.

2   **They are close to you.** Obviously it's difficult to do in a one day INSET, but an expert is one who comes alongside and mentors rather than lectures at a distance. They are willing to engage with

you and apply ideas to your situation. You feel that they actually want you to succeed.

3 **They are generous with their expertise**. They are not just there to do exactly what they are paid to do; they go the extra mile – a little bit like teachers.

What to listen to: dealing with expert comments

Teaching is at least as much an art as it is a science. Hence it is understandable that judging teaching is a complex business. Professor Robert Coe's study casts doubt on the ability of observers to correctly assess the quality of lessons. Where grade 1 (outstanding) was given, the probability that a second observer would give a different grade was between 51% and 78%. Surprisingly the inadequate lesson was even harder to spot: 90% of second observers would have given a different grade (Coe 2014). This is not surprising as learning, a little like the iceberg, is mostly below the surface. We may observe effects or evidence of it, but none of us can know exactly what is in the mind of another. In dealing with what is said to us:

1 **Challenge factual errors**. If something is said that is just not the case, point it out. If it is in a written observation document, ask for it to be taken out. If it is CPD, a discrete correction of the trainer in private afterwards may be required.

2 **If it is a matter of perception and perspective, offer the other side**. The observer may have seen the change of activity as indecisiveness; you saw it as responding to student voice. Similarly what is not said can also be important. In one observation a few years ago, whilst agreeing with the two main weaknesses the observer identified, I felt that a number of strengths had been overlooked and courteously presented the other side to my observer.

3 **Ask for thinking time or more information when you need it**. Sometimes an expert will present us with data that is new to us that we have not had time to process: 'Your Value Added score is X, which is 10% lower than similar providers, according to . . .' If you are

unsure about whether something is true or what the significance is, saying thank you but you will need to look at it in more detail is not unreasonable. On some occasions I have found that data presented in meetings has on closer inspection turned out to be false.

4 **Buy a saddle.** Of course there is often a nugget of truth in most feedback as much as we may not like it. If the same things are consistently said, then we have to take it on board and, to paraphrase Ben Kingsley's character in *Lucky Number Slevin*, if three people have said you are a horse, you may need to buy a saddle. Hence if three observers or inspectors have said that you should develop your questioning, at least consider it!

Whatever is said and however it is said, always be polite and professional. No matter how valid your point, you have lost the argument once you lose control. Try to be authentic and true to yourself.

Top tip: If you can't beat them . . .

Perhaps the best defence against the experts of education is to become one whilst remaining in the classroom. Keeping up to date with reading and research in the TES, on Twitter, on journals or by further study will at least enable you to see through some of the more empty pieces of advice or enable you to present a case on at least equal terms. Being informed and knowledgeable is the difference between being confident to challenge something and just accepting what you are told.

Leadership byte: gatekeeper

As a leader you cannot lock Ofsted out of a building, but you are the gatekeeper in terms of other experts. Try to get feedback from other institutions before inviting trainers and consultants in. As much as you don't want poor teaching, you equally do not want good staff confused or demoralised by pseudo-expertise. You are hopefully in a position to make sound judgements on quality yourself.

Questions for reflection

1 Are there areas that are identified regularly by observers or consultants whom you encounter? In which areas do you need to 'buy a saddle'?

2 How is your own expertise developing? What are you reading or listening to that will enable you to self-assess more accurately?

Bibliography

Coe, R (2014) *Classroom observation: It's harder than you think.* Available from www.cem.org/blog/414/ (Accessed 19th February 2016).

Chapter 39

An inspector calls – Ofsted and observation

If a teacher teaches a lesson in a classroom and no inspector is there to observe it, can it still be a good lesson?

This chapter has been rightly placed near the end of the book. As teachers we should not be doing anything solely to please Ofsted. It is important, as stated earlier, to keep our eyes on the ball not on the scoreboard; if we are doing things well and correctly, Ofsted will likely confirm that. If not, then our smoke and mirrors are unlikely to fool them. If, as some people believe, the data is all they are interested in, then the outcome is largely determined before they arrive. As I write the future of Ofsted looks uncertain; it is likely that a system of peer review or shorter inspections will replace what is currently there. Nevertheless, at present a visit from the inspectors can be a very stressful experience, as can any observation of your teaching. The level of panic and hysteria that can take place in an institution prior to an Ofsted has to be experienced to be believed. Recently I heard of one classroom teacher who was still taking phone calls and texts at 2:00 a.m. on the morning of an Ofsted from her stressed, micromanaging headteacher. This chapter looks at how we can reduce some of the stress from what is one of the most challenging aspects of teaching.

Long term planning

Realising that at some point you are going to be inspected, or at some point during the academic year you will be formally observed, means that you can get ahead with your planning if you are organised. Consider the following:

1   Make sure your key course documents are up-to-date. What are your policies? Are you following school policies? How? Have you got a scheme of work? Have you got an assessment plan? Although you may need to take half a day of a holiday or weekend to do this, it is time well spent once you get the call.

2   Keep a class file. This will have a record of marks and data on students. Your school or college may centralise this. Make sure that notes that an observer needs to be aware of are all kept prominently (e.g. John has autism. Natasha has suffered a bereavement and is prone to burst into tears when directly questioned. Salim has missed a month and is behind.) Add anything that affects how you teach and may not be immediately apparent to an observer.

3   Every now and then collect assessed work that you have marked thoroughly for a few different students with a range of abilities. This shows student progress and the detail of your feedback.

4   If there is an agreed lesson plan in your institution, it is probably best to use this for inspection. Find it before the call comes. However, it is worth noting that inspectors only require evidence of planning, not an actual lesson plan; the 5 minute lesson plans such as those advocated by @teachertoolkit should be fine.

As a bonus, if you are super keen – or having difficulty sleeping – download and read the latest Ofsted framework. Unfortunately inspection focuses often change like the wind so being aware of what the current buzzwords are can be useful.

Much of the above should be available electronically. If you have a decent electronic filing system, it shouldn't be too difficult to retrieve it in the event of the call. When we were last inspected, I was able to retrieve most of the information above, have it printed and compile it in an impressive folder within an hour.

Getting the call – fine tuning

Your lessons will of course be already more or less prepared. Remember that an inspection or an observation is to some extent like a driving test; there are certain things that may be subtle, but you will need to flag up to the observer. In fine tuning the lessons you have already planned, consider the following questions:

What do you want **them** to **achieve** and how will you **know** they have **all** done it?

What: Look at your learning objectives. Tweak your objectives if need be; they should state what the end of the lesson will look like. What will students be able to do?

Them: Remember the lesson is about learning not necessarily about clever activities. Look again at the lesson from the student point of view. Will they be learning and focused?

Achieve: Will what you have planned help weak learners to get somewhere? How will they be supported? How will more able learners be challenged? In other words, can you show differentiation?

Know: What assessment for learning strategies are you using to show whether students have made progress or not? Think how you might respond if learners are not progressing as expected. What is plan B?

All: Give some thought to directed questions and how you may be able to connect or speak to all learners within the observation. Will they all be involved and learning or might there be passengers?

Hopefully your existing plans can be fine-tuned but occasionally you look at a lesson and realise it will not suffice. Where a lesson needs reconstructing – use your go-to strategies. Do what students are familiar with and you have practiced; gimmicks to please Ofsted are likely to backfire.

Getting the call – intruder alert

When an inspector or observer walks in, although it's easier said than done, try not to panic. Remember to smile and direct them to where you would like them to sit. Be friendly. Remember that decisions are made at an emotional level. If you are prickly or stand-offish, it is harder for them to gain an emotional connection, and there is even some evidence that this can be a factor in inspectors coming to judgements!

Try to involve all students with direct questions or by checking their work. Where unexpected opportunities to link to numeracy of equality and diversity present themselves, pause what you are doing and take it. Above all have the confidence to move off plan if what you are doing is not working.

Try not to be overly concerned if the inspectors appear harsh initially. They often come in with a hypothesis to test and are looking for you to answer their initial questions and defend your position rather than cave in.

Troubleshooting

Occasionally things go wrong. If an inspector says something that is completely incorrect, challenge it and report it to your nominee – the member of your senior team who is dealing with the inspectors – just as you would challenge a factual error in an internal observation.

Equally if an inspector says something that is inappropriate, challenge it and report it. During one inspection I was part of, an inspector said to a colleague, 'When did you lose your passion for teaching your subject?' This was reported and an apology was made.

Finally

Give yourself something to look forward to when inspection is over. It could be a meal out with family, a few drinks with colleagues or a quiet night with a DVD. Allow yourself a treat to look forward to. You will also need extra sleep.

? **Questions for reflection**

1 If you got the call today, how ready are you? What can you do ahead of time do ensure you are prepared?

2 If you have to teach a good lesson at short notice, what are your go-to strategies and routines that your group are familiar with?

Chapter 40

And finally – top ten tips

If you are prone to skip to the end of books before reading, you may be disappointed with this final chapter. This is for those who have read all the way through; think of these points as an aide-memoire. Teaching is an incredibly fulfilling, yet ridiculously demanding, job. Surviving and flourishing in the classroom is demanding physically and mentally. Yet we can do things that will help ourselves. Increasingly wellbeing will become an issue for SLTs to consider as teacher shortages bite, but there are no magic wands. Our wellbeing is at least partly our responsibility. We can and must help ourselves and each other.

So when you forget everything else, remember:

1 **Well teachers teach well** – Wellbeing is not a side issue. Remember to manage energy just as much as you manage time. There are lots of demands on us as teachers, but we can't do any of them if we've collapsed in a heap somewhere. You are the number one resource that your students have.

2 **Teach well – and be confident**. Whatever is going on, our main priority is planning, teaching and marking. It is tempting to do limited preparation when we have a lot of other tasks to do, but this strategy backfires. If we teach well, it does wonders for our confidence and puts the admin into perspective. Teach badly and we become convinced that we are no good at anything. The number one priority and the thing that most affects our confidence is our teaching.

3 **Go easy on the guilt** – Try to keep it in perspective. So one particular lesson didn't go so well? You've not ruined the lives of those 30 young people; it's not the end of the world. There's another day tomorrow. Don't succumb to perfectionism; accept that you will never complete the list.

4 **Rest** – Physical and mental energy levels are important. Make sure yours are topped up. When you're shattered and drained, you will take twice as long doing things and probably do them badly. Take at least one midweek evening off completely and have at least one full day off at the weekend. Your energy levels are the most important thing in determining how things go in the classroom.

5 **Look after yourself – stay positive** – There will be those around you for whom the glass is forever half empty, and we are required to account for those things that didn't go so well. It's easy to overlook the fact that most things have gone well. Remind yourself of what you can do. Celebrate success.

6 **The long game** – Teaching is a long game: a marathon not a sprint. It's not about the first week or the second week. It's about the whole year in colleges or, in schools, several years. We would love to deliver outstanding lessons all the time, mark two essays for each student every week, run three after school clubs etc. but we have to be realistic. Being organised means hassle at the start of the year for long term gain.

7 **Stick to your values and principles** – Decide what matters and what doesn't. Try not to be moved. The question 'Why?' is the most powerful one you can ask. Remember your teacher SHAPE; some things are valid and good but not for you.

8 **Help** – Ask for help when you need it, and take advantage of any that is on offer. Just because we are often on our own in the classroom doesn't mean that we have to do everything on our own. Use the wider team and play your part in that team.

9 **Significant others** – Make time for family and friends. Remember that you are not just a teacher. Make sure your relationships stay healthy and strong. Don't be tempted to spend all the weekend in the spare room preparing. Have some time during which you are a person not just a teacher. That way you'll come into the classroom refreshed at the start of the week.

10　**Grow and have fun** – Finally, grow as a person and as a teacher. Try to be as good as you can at what you do, but remember that your mental health matters more. Look for things to enjoy each day; schools and colleges are quite often hilarious places.

Some days teaching will feel like the worst job in the world, but when things are going well it is the best. If we can remove some of the unnecessary nonsense and keep our minds relatively balanced and positive, then a long and fulfilling career can be ours.

Suggestions for further reading

ATL (2016) *Voice care.* ATL website. Available from https://www.atl.org.uk/health-and-safety/staff-and-pupil-issues/voice-care.asp (Accessed 14th February 2016).

Cowley, S (2009) *Teaching Skills for Dummies,* Chichester: John Wiley & Sons.

Dweck, C (2012) *Mindset: The New Psychology of Success,* New York: Robinson.

Goleman, D (1995) *Emotional Intelligence – Why It Can Matter More Than IQ,* New York: Bloomsbury.

Hilton, J (2016) *Leading from the Edge,* London: Bloomsbury.

Hybels, B (2008) *Axiom – Powerful Leadership Proverbs,* Zondervan: Michigan.

Kidd, D (2014) *Teaching: Notes from the Frontline,* Camarthen: Independent Thinking Press.

Lee, K (2013) *4 ways to look after your voice.* Available from http://www.katelee.co.uk/blog/4-ways-to-look-after-your-voice/ (Accessed 14th February 2016).

Lovewell, K (2012) *Every Teacher Matters,* Penryn: Ecademy Press.

Morrison McGill, R (2015) *Teacher Toolkit: Helping You Survive Your First 5 Years,* London: Bloomsbury.

Oakes, S and Griffin, M (2016) *The A Level Mindset – 40 Activities for Transforming Student Commitment, Motivation and Productivity,* Camarthen: Crown House.

Peters, S (2011) *The Chimp Paradox,* London: Vermilion.

Proctor, A and Proctor, E (2013) *The Essential Guide to Burnout: Overcoming Excess Stress,* Oxford: Lion Hudson.

Reah, M (2014) *Teacher 5 a day.* Available from https://martynreah.wordpress.com/2014/12/06/teacher5aday (Accessed 10th January 2016).

Rogers, W (1992) *Managing Teacher Stress,* London: Prentice Hall.

Rogers, W (2011) *The Essential Guide to Managing Teacher Stress,* Harlow: Longman.

Smith, J (2010) *The Lazy Teacher's Handbook,* Camarthen: Crown House.

Tomsett, J (2015) *This Much I Know about Love Over Fear,* Camarthen: Crown House.

Index